Ways of Knowing in Science and Mathematics Series

RICHARD DUSCHL, SERIES EDITOR

ADVISORY BOARD: Charles W. Anderson, Raffaella Borasi,
Nancy Brickhouse, Marvin Druger, Eleanor Duckworth, Peter Fensham,
William Kyle, Roy Pea, Edward Silver, Russell Yeany

Designing Everyday Assessment in the Science Classroom

J Myron Atkin
Janet E. Coffey
Savitha Moorthy
Mistilina Sato
Matthew Thibeault

Foreword by Gerry Wheeler

TEACHERS
COLLEGE
PRESS

Teachers College, Columbia University
New York and London

Published by Teachers College Press, 1234 Amsterdam Avenue, New York, NY 10027

The Classroom Assessment Project to Improve Teaching and Learning (CAPITAL) was funded by a grant from the National Science Foundation (REC-9909370). The grant also supported the partnership between CAPITAL, based at Stanford University, and the King's-Medway-Oxfordshire Formative Assessment Project centered at King's College London.

Library of Congress Cataloging-in-Publication Data

Designing everyday assessment in the science classroom / J Myron Atkin . . . [et al.] ;
   foreword by Gerry Wheeler.
      p. cm. — (Ways of knowing in science and mathematics series)
   Includes bibliographical references and index.
   ISBN 0-8077-4633-9 (alk. paper)
    1. Science—Study and teaching—United States—Evaluation. I. Atkin, J Myron.
II. Series.

  LB1585.3.D47 2005
  507.1'073—dc22   2005048602

ISBN-13: 978-0-8077-4633-2 (paper)   ISBN-10: 0-8077-4633-9 (paper)

Printed on acid-free paper
Manufactured in the United States of America

12 11 10 09 08 07 06 05   8 7 6 5 4 3 2 1

Contents

Foreword

THIS BOOK TAKES formative assessment to a new level. The authors give us a case study glimpse of a 4-year project in which active middle-level science teachers, in partnership with Stanford researchers, explored their everyday assessment strategies. In short, the book presents a delightfully rich set of images of science teachers searching for the "artifacts" of student understanding who, through the process, ultimately chart pathways for their teaching.

I suspect that if pressured, most science teachers would confess to having a fairly narrow view of classroom assessment: Many of us start our teaching careers thinking that the primary (if not the only) role of assessment is to assign a grade. Later, we consider formative assessment, but still with the goal of giving grades: testing our students more frequently early on in the course so that we and they can track their progress. (We feel it is our duty to alert those students who are likely to fail.) But assessments can be much more for the teacher as well as for the students. This book shows through its stories how teachers can use a variety of formative assessment techniques to answer questions they have about their teaching. Readers will not find much mention of giving grades.

The science teachers in the project were given much latitude in choosing their assessment focus. Some wrestled with peer assessment, self-assessment, ungraded assignments, writing and assessment, feedback, quizzes, reporting, and grading. One teacher who felt challenged by the apparent disengagement between test performance and understanding, for example, explored the validity of classroom responses. Should she view them as valid in the same sense as a test response? Another teacher asked if fairness meant that every learner would have the same chance to "win the race" or that every learner would receive the same chance to "finish the race." Does every student get the same treatment—the same uniform experience—or does he/she get what's needed to reach the same end result?

The richness came from the teachers' willingness to reflect on their efforts. Science teachers will enjoy this book because in its pages we can "observe" our colleagues in real-world settings. But the book also should be read by principals, science curriculum coordinators, and science department chairs. They, in their roles as "culture keepers" of the educational program, must get involved. They are the ones who can transform this externally funded experiment into an internally supported, high-quality professional development experience in their schools.

In the last chapter, the authors, appropriately, ask what has been learned and how this project could guide a scaled-up effort. I won't spoil your fun by summarizing their insights, but I will state the obvious: that it takes time and varies with context.

The reader will gain a unique and very special insight into the thinking of the teachers as they execute their "experiments." The project team—who first served as researcher partners with the teachers, noting the tensions each teacher faced, and later as authors of this book—do an excellent job of discussing individually the many factors involved in active, reflective teaching.

In the end, the one message that stands out is that reflective teaching is a highly personal matter. Each teacher chose a question, and all of the teachers grew professionally, but in different ways. As one teacher put it, "It's almost scary how you can teach this many years and then suddenly feel like [you're] jumping off a cliff or something."

With this well-written book, readers will gain new insights into everyday assessment by following the experiences of six teachers as they approach their assessment experiments. It's a rich story of teachers changing. And the reader gets to see how the tensions among context, content, and the personal are resolved in classroom assessments.

—Gerry Wheeler
Executive Director, National Science Teachers Association

The Local and the Practical: Examining Teachers' Assessment Practices in the Science Classroom

THE POINT OF any attempt to modify educational practice and policy is to influence what happens when teachers and students work together in classrooms. Everything else is secondary. Research, especially during the past 15 years, points consistently and strongly to the conclusion that a particularly effective way to enrich that experience, and improve learning, is to help teachers improve the assessment practices they employ day by day in their own classrooms (see, e.g., Black & Wiliam, 1998a; Crooks, 1988).

Ongoing assessment linked to improved student learning reaches beyond grading practices and test design to include activities that are integrated into regular, everyday classroom activity. This everyday classroom assessment entails taking the steps necessary to identify the gap between a student's current work and the desired aim—then together figuring out how the gap might be bridged. The research literature is replete with specific approaches: Listen carefully to what the student says. Wait several seconds for a student to respond to a question before proceeding with the discussion. Provide students with detailed feedback focused on how their work might be improved. Include opportunities for them to act on this feedback. Encourage students to discuss criteria for judging the quality of a report or presentation. Give them practice in discussing and assessing the quality of their own work and that of their peers. Find out how accurate they are about their own grasp of a particular concept, and how confident they are about that judgment. And that list is far from exhaustive. There is no one best form that assessment supportive of learning should take, but it occurs regularly and is integrated into everyday teaching activities.

Everyday classroom assessment practices are often difficult to distinguish from teaching. Assessment occurs whenever the focus is on the quality of student work, which happens several times an hour in many classrooms. It is a ubiquitous feature of every teacher's repertoire. This volume emphasizes how the information gleaned in analyzing student work and in classroom discussions of quality can be used more systematically to support student learning. While assessment activities arise in almost every classroom hour, the information obtained in the process—by the students and the teacher—is not consistently and constructively incorporated into instruction in a fashion that helps students do better work. Furthermore, students are not often involved in the assessment process, although such involvement is key to their becoming independent learners. This book reports how several teachers, over 3 years, tried to establish stronger links between assessment and student learning, and the challenges they faced.

Like almost all other aspects of teaching, assessment is resistant to change. And like many other aspects of teaching, effecting change requires more than introducing or implementing particular strategies or protocols. How teachers go about modifying their varying assessment practices goes to the heart of how they view their role as teachers. Teaching has always been a personal act. Examining just what kind of relationship they want with their students raises basic and profound personal questions for teachers. Teachers are judges and arbiters. They are coaches and guides. They are also models and exemplars. Who teachers are and wish to be, and how they wish to be seen as professionals—by their students, by the community, and by themselves—are driving forces that propel the decisions they make every day in their classrooms. These aspects of teachers' sense of themselves inform how they integrate their multiple and possibly competing roles, or choose not to. Understanding and capitalizing upon the personal nature of teaching becomes central to meaningful and long-term professional growth.

CLASSROOM ASSESSMENT PROJECT TO IMPROVE TEACHING AND LEARNING (CAPITAL)

The compelling research in the realm of classroom assessment that suggests both the strength of improved classroom assessment and the paucity of effective practice, combined with the recognition of the personal nature of teaching, provided the stimulus and foundation for the Classroom Assessment Project to Improve Teaching and Learning (CAPITAL). CAPITAL was launched to probe deeply into teacher change with regard to classroom assessment. The National Science Foundation (NSF) supported the 4-year effort to study how teachers shape and modify their practices to create the conditions for the kind of assessment that fosters learning. We set out to investigate how more than 25 teachers grappled with both personal and professional challenges—for the two are inseparable—to try to become the kind of the teachers they wanted to be. We tried to learn about what each one did to shape the "assessment culture" in his or her classroom. We were guided by such questions as, What are the assessment practices of each teacher? How are they developed? How do teachers actually improve their day-by-day assessment efforts to enhance students' learning? And how might a research team from Stanford University lend a hand?

With these questions as guides, researchers from Stanford immersed themselves in the classrooms and conversations of participating teachers. We spent time in classrooms, talked with teachers and students extensively, convened monthly meetings of the teachers, and facilitated week-long summer institutes for all the participants.

THE CAPITAL STANCE

Certain convictions about teachers and teaching guided the CAPI-TAL research. While we struggled at times with what these views and convictions meant in our work, they remained central in discussions, decisions, and day-to-day involvement with teachers.

Every member of the Stanford group had been a classroom teacher. All of us had grappled with the necessity of making big and small decisions to increase our own effectiveness with students. We knew that teachers, like all people with real-world responsibilities, tailor their day-to-day work to the circumstances in which they find themselves. Good teaching is not a scripted activity. The specific context matters. So does opportunity. While the acts of any teacher usually have a general flow, pattern, and direction—depending partly on the teacher's own knowledge, predilections, experience, and beliefs—unpredictable and unavoidable circumstances *always* arise. Teachers must cope continually with challenges that have little precedent, either in their profession or in their personal experience.

Our collective experience led us to the conviction that in trying to understand teachers and help them improve their work, it was as important to comprehend the variations among them as to identify the similarities. It is true that one inevitably looks for patterns to make sense of the world. And a great deal is known about how students learn and how teachers teach; some powerful theories illuminate and help guide good practice. But the variations among teachers and the circumstances in which they work are significant. In fact it is in their individuality that teachers often have the greatest influence on their students, as anyone who has ever been either a teacher or a student knows. It is partly by trying to fathom some of these variations among teachers, we believe, that the most salient programs for professional development could be developed.

Consequently we were intent in our research on finding out as much as we could about each teacher as an individual and the assumptions and theories that guide and frame the contours of that teacher's professional practice. These guiding theories are often practical: that is, they are directed toward action in particular circumstances. They can be dynamic, changing and evolving over time, or they can be long-held views that consistently guide the work of the teacher. While they can be influenced by more general theory, they often are more concrete than abstract. They aim to be timely rather than timeless. They must be prudent, within highly particularized circumstances, so they draw at least as much on local knowledge as on general principles. They are shaped by the teachers' beliefs about education, about themselves, and about their students. They are powerfully influenced by the teacher's own values, experiences, and sense of the possible. They are continuallyshaped, reshaped, and affirmed through action and reflection.

Our theoretical framework assumes that teachers make decisions for reasons. In our work, we sought to identify and understand what guides a teacher's daily activity. What "practical" theories can be identified as teachers engage in their daily practice? How were Louise's assessment practices during the years we worked with her influenced by her many years working in a science laboratory? How were Anthony's actions in the classroom shaped by his decade-long position as a teacher and teacher leader in Oakland? What led Jen to the view that she could not separate assessing her students' science knowledge from dealing directly with their ability to convey their ideas in writing—and that she had to teach science *and* writing to make fair and useful judgments about what her students knew and the help they needed? What challenges did Irene need to overcome as she sought to shift the focus of her classroom away from letter grades, which she came to understand as sometimes counterproductive?

Our effort to understand why the teacher took particular actions was a powerful factor in our day-by-day activities in the project. We set out to work *with* the teachers and approached each one's professional world as unique. We tried to cultivate a reflective orientation toward teaching, particularly as we engaged teachers in efforts to examine their own practices. Teachers identified aspects of their daily activity that they wanted to improve or learn more about with respect to assessment, tried new strategies or approaches that they thought might work for their students in their own settings, and came together regularly to talk about the developments in their classrooms. Researchers observed and supported the teachers' own classroom inquiries, and prompted them to articulate their developing understanding for themselves, for us, and for one another. CAPI-TAL provided collaborative opportunities during formal monthly meetings, informally connecting teachers with similar interests.

We also started as a project specifically attuned to issues of assessment. We drew generously on the classroom assessment literature that discussed assessment *for* learning, and on the work of Paul Black and Dylan Wiliam (1998a, 1998b) and their colleagues and collaborators (Black, Harrison, Lee, Marshall, & Wiliam, 2002) in particular. This view stands in contrast to more conventional views of assessment, in which emphasis is placed on summative tests, or an assessment *of* learning. (CAPITAL received support from the National Science Foundation for establishing close relationships with Black and Wiliam at King's College London.) We went into our work defining assessment broadly to include all the activities undertaken by teachers and students that help identify the nature of student understanding, and how that knowledge feeds into teaching and learning. We shared research with teachers when relevant, but left it up to the teachers to determine the forms and focus assessment took in their classrooms.

Teasing assessment apart from the many other strands of teacher practice with which it is so tightly interwoven proved challenging and seemed forced. Assessment that supports learning is so tightly coupled with other teaching activities that making a distinction at times appeared artificial. Yet herein lay its strength. The very density of those connections—to teaching, learning, and curriculum—makes assessment a particularly productive focus for professional development opportunities. It provides a lens for examining a full range of issues that are important for the teacher, and encourages the teacher to integrate them. Still, the degree to which assessment itself was emphasized varied from teacher to teacher and from month to month.

ORGANIZATION OF THE BOOK

This chapter has introduced many of the theoretical predispositions that guided our work, highlighting our stance on the personal nature of change. In the chapters that follow, we hope to ground these

ideas in the classrooms and lives of our teachers, and raise new issues that will be taken up later. When relevant, we provide the kind
of detail that honors the complexity of the classroom. We embed
analysis within the chapters, and highlight variation as it helps illuminate a dilemma or emphasize a point.

In Chapters 2 and 3 we identify and explore the practical theories that become salient as teachers engage in their daily practice.
In doing so, we try to capture the interaction and interplay among
personal experiences and background, context, and action. Chapter 2 centers on two teachers' use of student work as central to their
classroom assessment practices. We consider how Jen and Louise
examined student work, and discuss how their views of science
inform their analysis and subsequent actions. Their perspectives on
the nature of science are enmeshed with their views about their students and their students' needs, the purpose of the assignment, and
classroom constraints that shape their work.

In Chapter 3, we take a broader and deeper look at a personal
trajectory of change that spanned the course of this project. Each of
the participating teachers presents a unique personal and professional trajectory. All are going somewhere, and have their own goals,
dreams, and aspirations as to who they want to be as teachers, where
they want to go, and what they want their classrooms to look like.
The story of Irene in Chapter 3 aims to capture how her participation in CAPITAL moved her in the direction of her vision, and how
this vision shifted as she participated in this project. Irene's journey was not always smooth, nor was it linear. Change was deliberate and occurred slowly; it was frustrating and at times painful.

Chapter 4 takes up issues of collaboration and provides a look
at the sequence of events that occurred when a small group of
teachers who worked closely with one another in the same school
district came together around an examination of practice. In this
chapter, we consider the features that gave rise to their productive and powerful relationships. The teachers' experiences and
reflections raise important questions for design of professional development and dissemination.

As professionals, all our teachers were driven by opportunities
they saw to make a difference. These opportunities were not focused
solely on classroom practices. While many of the teachers sought

to make an immediate impact on the experience of students by focusing on their work in the classroom, others sought changes elsewhere, as well. They initiated and were drawn to district reform initiatives, primarily to ones involving work with other teachers. They were community activists, seeking to make an impact beyond the walls of their classrooms. We had not anticipated these directions for their work with assessment, and at times struggled to make sense of these emphases in light of the aims for the overall project. In one instance, our approach of focusing on action in the classroom proved less effective as an entry point to change than anticipated. Chapter 5 considers these additional dimensions in the life of a teacher.

One aim of CAPITAL was to explore the professional development approaches we employed, and in particular, to examine their possible relevance to discussions of how effective practices spread in the broader educational community. In Chapter 6, we revisit our theoretical roots and orientations and elaborate on challenges we faced along the way. In Chapter 7, we briefly make some recommendations that flow from our experiences and, in the process, raise questions about several conventional notions of dissemination. In honoring the personal priorities, visions, and unique contexts in which teachers work, we raise questions about many strategies to "scale up" effective practice. Thus Chapter 7 returns to actual classroom practice and offers some concrete suggestions for facilitating change that place teachers at the center of efforts to improve their own practices.

INTRODUCTION TO THE TEACHERS

Before we enter specific classrooms, we want to note that the teachers with whom we worked in CAPITAL were extraordinary in ordinary ways. Some were new to the profession, many had been teaching for 10 to 15 years, and several found their way to teaching after other careers. They were stretched thin with commitments as they juggled multiple responsibilities in the midst of a system that was placing increasing demands and numerous constraints on their work. Nevertheless, they were all deeply committed to their work as teachers. They cared passionately about students and their subject areas, and struggled with how best to help their diverse groups of students learn.

The accounts in this book highlight the activities of a small number of the teachers with whom we worked. We introduce them here briefly, and leave their stories to be told in the chapters that follow. Irene, Joe, and Louise all teach in the San Francisco Unified School District. At the time this book was completed, Irene had been at the same middle school for 11 years, and Joe had been in the district for more than a decade. Louise, a former lab biologist, had taught at her school for 6 years. Anthony and Caleb taught in the Oakland Unified School District, a school district that went through a state takeover for its patterns of alleged mismanagement during the time we worked with them. Anthony had been a middle school teacher for 15 years, while Caleb had taught for 5 years. Jen was relatively new to the profession. A teacher of just 3 years when we started work with her, she taught at a tuition-free private school in East Palo Alto. The school was committed to preparing all of its students for college entrance, and many of them would be the first in their families to attend college. Vicki, Tracey, Joni, Elaine, and Neil taught in the New Haven Unified School District, a district that serves a diverse community south of Oakland.

CAPITAL had two prongs. We embarked on a research project centered on change in classroom assessment, and also intent on considering issues of professional development. What emerged through the process was a collaborative effort among teachers and researchers, with dimensions of research and professional development for both the classroom teachers and project staff. This book contains the stories of a few of these journeys.

Learning from Student Work: Jen and Louise

MOTIVATED LARGELY BY her own uninspiring experiences as a student, Jen felt strongly that it was her responsibility as a teacher to "turn her students on to science" ("I just want them to have this sense of wonder about it") and to create opportunities for them to have an "oh my gosh, this world is so amazing!" moment. Her ideas about how students should pursue learning in an ideal classroom environment were broad: "I want them to learn how to learn about things that interest them and I want to expose them to things they may have not ever known about." Jen believed in learning by active engagement; besides actually "doing" things, she thought, students learned best "when they're interested and when they feel like they have some control over what they are doing." Consequently, she believed that students should be independent and that, as a teacher, it was her role to help students take ownership and responsibility for their own learning.

Louise described much of school science as fostering mastery of factual information that was superficial, short-lived, and at times unimportant and inaccurate. She was much more interested in how science understanding was achieved, modified, shared, and revised: "The important thing I hope to do is to get students thinking about what science really is." Inspired by her philosophical orientation and past experience as a practicing scientist, she felt herself most successful when she was able to change her mind. In the same way, a prominent goal for her as a teacher was to provide opportunities and support for her students to change their minds as they studied science in her classroom: "For me, changing your mind is the best kind of learning. This was like real science to me. This is how scientists work. . . . What I want to do from now on is really focus on teaching towards changing [the students'] minds because that is so powerful."

This chapter follows the stories of Jen and Louise as they charted their unique courses toward being and becoming teachers who were reflective about their teaching and assessment, and specifically as they explored the question, How do we know what we know about students' understanding? Given this question, each teacher found it necessary to pay careful attention to the work students did in their classroom. Louise looked for evidence of student understanding and indications of a "change in mind." Jen's use of student work challenged her assumptions about what understanding means and looks like—and led her to a more nuanced view of how language itself was tightly intertwined with science content in her students' writing.

ARTICULATING UNDERSTANDING THROUGH WRITING: A STORY FROM JEN'S CLASSROOM

Jen's goal for her students was that they understand science concepts with which they could become engaged, both physically and intellectually; her classroom called for active involvement with both objects and ideas. She was disappointed, however, by the limited ability of many of her students to describe what they were seeing and thinking, especially in writing. How could she begin to comprehend what they actually knew if they had problems conveying their ideas? Since she was not teaching them to write, she felt strongly that she could not hold them accountable for their writing or the understanding of science they conveyed through written work:

> My students don't really like to write. They don't like to explain fully in writing. So they'll talk fully and explain in talking, but when I make them write a lot I get a very abbreviated answer. And I don't know if it is my role really to

teach [writing]. I mean I have to teach them some ways of explaining themselves, but I'd rather do other things. I'd rather talk to them and hear their understanding than limit their understanding because their writing is hindering them.

In preparation for a week-long meeting of all CAPITAL participants in the summer of 2001, the Stanford-based staff asked each of the teachers to bring a collection of student work to share with the others, so that the group could discuss evidence of student understanding. As Jen went over her students' portfolios at the end of the school year to select pieces of work, her doubts began to crystallize about her students' grasp of science content as it was reflected in their writing. She questioned more acutely the questionable relationship she saw between what students took away from her classroom in terms of understanding and what they articulated when they were required to write. How could she as a teacher determine the nature of that relationship? As she put it much later, "My students' writing raised a very important question: Do they not know the science well enough to clearly explain it? Or do they not know the mechanics of good, clear writing? . . . Poorly written science answers didn't help me assess their understanding of science."

At the same time that Jen brought these questions to the entire group, she also spent time with her co-teacher reflecting on the year that had passed and setting goals for the year ahead. They concluded that they had not emphasized communication sufficiently as an important goal in their classrooms, and they resolved to devote more time to the subject. Discussions with her co-teacher and her CAPITAL colleagues during the summer thus converged somewhat serendipitously to expand Jen's goals to incorporate teaching the students to articulate more clearly what they understood and to focus on writing in her classroom.

HOW ARE THINKING AND WRITING LINKED?
COMING TO A NEW UNDERSTANDING

At the start of the project, Jen had seen understanding of science and writing about it in an easy correspondence. "If they understand it, they'll be able to write about it," she remarked to a researcher from

Stanford early in the first year of the project. With closer examination of her students' work over the course of several months of project-stimulated conversations, she became aware that the relationship between conceptual understanding and its expression in writing was not as uncomplicated as she had imagined.

During a curricular unit on the digestive system, for example, Jen assigned her students the task of writing a travel guide to the digestive system. For this they were asked to model their writing on a travel brochure and write for an imaginary audience that would one day travel through this bodily system. In addition, they had to include factual descriptions that detailed the organs and the roles they played in the job of digestion.

This assignment was divided into several segments, and students worked on it for many weeks, organ by organ. To support her students in this exercise, Jen prepared a requirements sheet that listed vocabulary to use and define, as well as other features that they would need to write about to complete the assignment, such as instructions on "what to pack," "what to do or see," and "pictures/map." She explained the assignment to a group of CAPITAL teachers and researchers: "They had to write a paragraph explaining the role of the small intestine in digestion. And they had the vocabulary that they had to use, that I chose, saying that if you can use these words correctly . . . these are all the big parts of what the small intestine does."

When Jen looked at drafts of student work, she was struck by the uneven quality of their writing:

> Some paragraphs are really . . . accurate, and they're slow and they start out with a topic sentence. . . . Maybe, it's that it is logical and the order of the way things are written shows that there is some process of understanding. And this one [referring to another piece of work] to me is more of a laundry list of definitions just put together in a paragraph form. I didn't read this and say, yeah, the student has an understanding of what's going on.

In discussion of these work samples with CAPITAL colleagues, Jen focused on the work of one particular student, Jose, a seventh grader. Here is what he wrote:

The small intestine digests and absorbs the molecules in the food. *Villi* increase the *absorption* on the *surface area* in the small intestine while *diffusion* is happening. Diffusion is movement of molecules such as nutrients gas and oxygen moving from an area of high concentration to an area of low concentration. *Bile* is green *and* it helps break down fat and is stored in the *gall bladder*. The *liver* make bile. *Chyme* is a semifluid mixture of digestive juice and partially digested food. *Peristalsis* is the process that moves food through the gastro-intestinal tract. *Neutralization* is not letting the acids in the stomach work correctly. *Pancreas* contains a lot of powerful enzymes.

A SCIENCE TEACHER TURNS HER ATTENTION TO WRITING

Her examination of student work and what it revealed about student understanding persuaded Jen that, in addition to science content, it was her responsibility to deal with writing skills—after all, she was holding students accountable for written articulation of their understanding of science concepts in formulating her assessments. Although as a science and math teacher, she felt underprepared for the task, Jen took her students through several exercises that would help them write in a way that communicated their ideas more effectively. She wrote in a reflection at the end of the school year:

> I wanted my students to articulate their understanding in writing, but I worried that they lacked the skills to write clearly and effectively. I also worried that I lacked the skills to teach writing since it was outside my area of expertise. But if I was going to hold my students accountable for their writing, I needed to help them learn how to write better. So I began using writing lessons as one way to teach science content. This choice to focus on writing involved some compromises. I reluctantly included more time to revise drafts in class and less time doing hands-on activities, and as a result, worried that class would be less engaging for my students, and for me.

Initially my students had a lot of trouble writing information in logical order, which made it very difficult to determine how correctly they were thinking about the science. My students and I discussed how to write strong sentences and how to organize them into solid paragraphs. We did activities where students had to build paragraphs using sentences written on index cards.

Issues of both writing mechanisms and content began to surface in the way science was taught in Jen's classroom. In addition to having a topic sentence and supporting evidence, Jen's teaching began to include elements such as clarity of information, defining words and using them appropriately in context, and knowing how much information was adequate for explanation. She also began engaging her students in discussion about what makes a particular piece of writing "good," the difference between when something was correctly written and when it was clearly written, and what it meant to write creatively without compromising accuracy. This shift in focus is reflected in the following exchange with her students.

JEN: So, now, what are we going to do? What are you guys going to do before you turn in your final draft to make sure that what you think is clear really is clear to somebody else?

STUDENT 1: At first, read the paragraph, and then, after you read it, look at what the requirements are. Look through your paragraph. . . . Scan your paragraph to see if you have all the requirements.

STUDENT 2: You could have a friend read it and tell you if they understand it.

JEN: You could have a friend read it. Okay, . . .

STUDENT 3: I was going to say, like, you could show it to someone, like a sixth grader or someone who hasn't learned about that kind of stuff, and they could read and read it to see if it makes any sense.

STUDENT 4: When they read it, they can actually visualize being there. When you, like, say, what to see, and you're, like, describing the uvula, and if you describe it in, like, great detail, and you give them lots of things like how it looks and things that it does, when somebody, when they actually can, like, visualize what the uvula looks like, like, I'm taking a trip through the mouth, I'm looking at the uvula and they can visualize what it looks like, then, I think then, that means that you had explained it clearly.

JEN: Are you guys all getting one possible strategy that you could do before you give me your draft, your final project on Wednesday? Do you think it's better to give your paper to someone who knows something about digestion or to someone who doesn't know anything about digestion?

STUDENT 5: To somebody that does know.

JEN: Why?

STUDENT 5: Because, like, they will know, like, what, how it looks an' everything and since they did it so they can tell you if they think it's clearly written, they can tell you, like, did you explain it well enough, they can suggest what you should change.

JEN: We have an important idea, that the facts that you include in your travel guide need to be correct and somebody who understands digestion may be able to judge whether they are correct or not. We actually have two things going here: We have whether it's written clearly and whether it's written correctly.

As Jen brainstormed with her students about possible strategies they could use to assess and improve their writing, students learned to tease apart notions of accuracy and clarity as they applied them to a piece of writing.

The focus on writing also became evident in the type of feedback she provided to her students.

I read drafts of their writing, offered feedback, and students revised their work. Writing meaningful feedback on students' first drafts was a very laborious process because students had difficulty organizing their ideas. I had to write feedback about the mechanics of writing as well as the science content;

it was unclear whether feedback on the science, on their writing, or both would be the most beneficial to their learning.

I wrote planning outlines for questions to scaffold the paragraphs so students could organize their writing better. This added structure made it easier for me to see what my students understood about the content. As a result, my feedback became more directed at their understanding or misunderstanding of the science.

She found that it was important to give her students specific feedback on their early drafts that directed them to take some action:

The comments that you write need to give kids something to do. Rather than writing a question in the margin, it makes more sense to give them something to do, to make it an action thing, which they can read and feel, "This is what I need to do." . . .

It's a really different dialogue than when I'm reading something and giving thoughtful feedback, that they can read and do something with rather than say, "This part was wrong." And they recognize the difference now—they know when they get feedback that they don't know what to do with.

Thoughtful feedback, for Jen, began to take the form of comments on student writing like these:

- You need to explain the connection between absorption and diffusion before you explain diffusion
- Does the appendix have a role? Did it at one time? Put the sentence about the appendix here.
- This paragraph is all one sentence. Break into more than one sentence

After 8 days of focusing on writing, Jen showed us a revised version of the same student's, Jose's, paragraph on the small intestine. While Jose's revision still fell short of what she expected, she described it as being "so much better."

The small intestine digests and absorbs molecules in the food. It is 6 meters long and it is long because that is the biggest step of digestion so it needs a lot of room. The chyme flows through the small intestine and it goes there by peristalsis. There is a green liquid called bile that is in the small intestine that breaks down fat. It is made by the liver and stored in the gall bladder. There are enzymes in the small intestine that help digest food and they come from the pancreas when it shoots out pancreatic juices. When the chyme comes in the small intestine, neutralization happens and that is when the pancreatic juices stop the burning of the acids in the chyme so they won't burn a hole in the small intestine. There are finger-like projections in the small intestine called Villi, and the Villi increase the surface area and allow more nutrients to be move around from a high area of concentration to an area of low concentration and that is diffusion, then the nutrients gets absorbed in the Villi and it gets diffused in the bloodstream.

Jen felt that the way Jose wrote his description suggested that he understood the path of food through the digestive system and the function of the system's parts.

USING STUDENT WORK AS DATA TO SCAFFOLD CONCEPTUAL UNDERSTANDING: A STORY FROM LOUISE'S CLASSROOM

Committed to "set(ting) up conditions where students can change their minds and capture that change for themselves and for me," Louise aimed to provide experiences for students that help them confront and challenge their assumptions. She acknowledged that changing one's mind does not occur easily or overnight. Therefore her curriculum was designed to give students repeated opportunities to experience phenomena so that they might develop a richer understanding of concepts with each exposure.

A key dimension of Louise's assessment practice included looking for evidence of a change of mind in the work that her students produced, so she built in opportunities for them to record shifts in their ideas. The students' learning journals and their written responses to her Question of the Day were important sources. Through the Question of the Day, which students responded to at the start of each class period, Louise sought to promote reflection or elicit current understanding of a concept she saw as central to the unit at hand. In their journals, students wrote every night about the ideas they were developing and the ways in which they were changing their minds. These reflections included a description of what they did during class and how they did it, and what helped and/or hindered the lesson. They also wrote about their learning: what they already knew, what was new, and what they changed their minds about. In the third component of these nightly reflections, they paid attention to what they might need to learn next—what they didn't understand and what they would like to know more about.

In previous years, Louise had graded the students' learning journals and their responses to the daily question on the basis of accuracy. During her first year with CAPITAL, she reflected on the nature of assignments that seemed to generate the most useful information for her, and decided that she needed fuller responses to make adequate assessments. She wanted them to "take more risks," and believed they would do so more readily if they were not trying to figure out the exact response she was looking for and when they were not overly concerned with "getting it right." When she was grading for accuracy in the preceding year, she sensed her students were telling her what they thought she wanted to hear, often mimicking her use of language. Since she had ample opportunities to evaluate accuracy with other assessments, she altered her grading policy for the learning journals and Question of the Day responses. For these regular assignments, she began to assess the work on completion and progress (in essence, on effort). This change in policy made her more attentive to the questions she asked. She wanted them to generate the type of information she needed to draw reasonable inferences about students' understanding. A look at the work that students produced with this change in policy pleased Louise:

> I think the effort-only assessment is going well. I seem to be getting very long and involved responses from almost all of

my students. I don't remember having this much information last year. I can really plan the next day's lesson based on what the students already seem to know, or I can address common misconceptions. I am careful to avoid giving out the "right answer" to minitasks except through the lesson. (One student is complaining in his journal that he wants to know the answers.) My seventh graders are saying a lot and don't seem to mind hardly at all when their prior knowledge is later changed [about such questions] as "What is water made of?" and "What happens when water becomes so cold that it freezes?" For the question about water freezing, most thought that it would "look like" less water and were stunned when the ice was above their marking.

USING STUDENT WORK TO ADJUST TEACHING

A topic that Louise visited several times during the school year involved data collection and analysis. As a former scientist, she believed that understanding data was integral to understanding science. In her curriculum, she paid special attention to the notion of variation; in her opinion, it was one of the most crucial and most misunderstood scientific concepts. Specifically, she wanted her students to understand that "measurement has inherent inaccuracies (variation) that can be minimized." In small groups, students measured different objects and distances, using a variety of tools (spring scales, rulers, stopwatches) with a variety of scales (millimeters, centimeters, seconds, hundredths of seconds). They constructed histograms of their measurements, pooled information to reflect on their data and the process of gathering them, and discussed the variation that arose.

Shortly after they had covered the topic in the curriculum, students began to use the phrase "good data varies [*sic*]" confidently to explain variation in collected data. Initially, Louise was pleased; her students had grasped a difficult concept that was central to science. But her pleasure didn't last long.

A few days later, she provided students with a sample of data and asked them to discuss it. Several argued that it was good *because* it varied. Hearing the students' comments, she was no longer convinced that her students understood the main point, even though they had the language she had been listening for and were able to use it in contexts that made sense. From this episode, in conjunction with other assessment events, such as class work, homework, and quizzes, she concluded she still had work to do to help students understand variation and its role in science.

Observations of students' written work and their remarks in class led Louise to recognize that most of her students could identify human error as a source of variation. This idea in and of itself was not problematic, yet the frequency of this response raised flags with her. She knew that in the past, teachers had emphasized human error as the primary source of error. She wanted her students to realize that variation is a feature of data and that data vary even when collected by "the best, most careful scientists" using the most accurate instruments.

When she looked closely at their work, Louise saw little evidence that students understood what was meant by "good data vary"—the language they had quickly picked up—much less understood the explanations other than human error for why this would be the case. She used a Question of the Day prompt to catalyze reflection among students and to provide her with insight into what sense students were making of variation. She asked, "If we all measured the length of a snake, what would the histogram look like?" Her students provided a range of responses, primarily identifying sources of human error, as she had anticipated. But one student's work caught her eye:

> It would depend on if the snake was alive or dead. If it was dead the spread would be smaller. But if it was alive, the spread would be wider because it would move and might be a threat and become agitated and no one really wants to be holding an angry snake for enough time to be very accurate.

She commented that this explanation showed an understanding that data vary for reasons beyond human error. This student's response indicated to her that he understood that the actual object could contribute to variation in measurement. It showed he understood histograms and the marking of spreads. Human error was implied, but not as the only source of variation. Louise used this response as a springboard for conversation with her classes. "Why," she asked her students, "was this response a good one?" She wanted them to identify that many objects are difficult to measure, either because they move or because they are very large or very small.

SAMPLING STUDENT WORK TO GUIDE TEACHING

Louise saw her students' work as the best means for her own learning. She was guided by a single premise: "Assuming that the students were basically logical, there must have been a reason for their thinking." As she examined student work, Louise looked for trends in understanding, explanations, and reasoning. In the previous example, she grew skeptical at the ease with which students said, "Good data varies [sic]," and blamed herself for providing them with a sound bite that could distract them from really understanding a concept. She also identified "outliers" in student work, responses that represented what she would consider a particularly good understanding, or an interesting alternative explanation that could be addressed through her curriculum. Louise often posted these responses on the wall, as she did with the student's response to the "measuring the snake" question. She knew that her students would return to the idea of variation later in the year, and wanted them to be reminded of what they could learn from one another's responses.

The class, rather than the individual student, was Louise's unit of analysis. She decided which questions to consider more closely and sampled responses to get a sense of the general tendencies toward what students understood in her classroom. Whenever time permitted, Louise often recorded selected responses to daily questions in the form of a table. At other times, as she went over student responses, she made tally marks on a scrap of paper (e.g., the number of times students mentioned what she would call a misconception, such as the phrase "going up or down hill" when describing a graph generated at a motion machine). When she came to an actual piece of student work that exemplified what she considered understanding, she hung the work on the classroom wall for other students to see. When a number of students missed the same item on a test or when she discovered a pattern to their responses, she examined interpretations she had not considered and tried to address them in her teaching.

Why did Louise seem less focused on the individual student? With time constraints associated with teaching five classes and more than 180 students, Louise did not have the time or energy to analyze every piece of work. She was forced to become selective. She sampled strategically and efficiently, as she had when she worked in a biotechnology firm. Louise's decision to use the class as the unit of analysis did not stem from practical considerations alone. As a rule, she was hesitant to make inferences about individuals. She was more comfortable saying that a piece of work exemplified a certain conceptual understanding, rather than stating that a student did or did not understand something. As Louise repeatedly asserted, "The absence of evidence is *not* evidence of absence." She was comfortable with the ambiguity that accompanied this stance. She was comfortable not always knowing what her students understood. She was comfortable saying that grades do not serve as a proxy for level of understanding (and on occasion challenged those who said that they can and/or do). And she was comfortable moving forward with new activities or onto a new unit when she was aware of a lack of clarity or had identified an area of confusion. One reason for her ease with this ambiguity lay in her belief that she was never really in a position to know with complete certainty what her students did and did not understand, nor was she convinced that understanding was static.

Thus her orientation towards curricula and teaching allowed her to be comfortable moving on before everybody "got it." She deliberately organized curriculum in a way that would allow students to experience and return to many "big ideas." She knew that students would be exposed to the same concepts across the course of the year in many different contexts and from different perspectives. She saw her role as not being solely to prepare her students for high school in the sense that she needed to expose and "cover" topics her students would need as they pursued science. Rather, she wanted her students to be prepared to do and to learn science, as she had done in the lab.

DIFFERENCES BETWEEN JEN AND LOUISE

It seems clear that Jen and Louise began their work in CAPITAL with different assumptions about their roles as teachers and different visions for how students should learn in their classrooms. Since the focus of CAPITAL was assessment, we made particular note of how they tried to improve this aspect of their practice, particularly as it might assist student learning. Both teachers used student work to acquire information that moved them towards somewhat different goals. To simplify somewhat, Jen used student work to see *if* her students understood. Louise used student work to see *what* they understood. Thus Jen's use of student work focused on the individual student's understanding. She cared about knowing where the particular student was in terms of grasping the concepts that were covered in the classroom *and* in terms of articulating that understanding in writing.

Louise, on the other hand, looked for classwide trends. Louise was less concerned with using student work to represent any single individual's level of understanding. She was much more interested in it as a way to make sense of the effectiveness of her own teaching, and as data that informed the day-to-day decisions she made in the classroom about what to teach and how to teach it. She drew on multiple sources, not so much to make a judgment about the quality of a student's work or inform a grade but rather to draw inferences about the class and to guide her own actions.

For both Jen and Louise, careful analysis of student work illuminated their underlying values and their priorities about what students should learn. For both Jen and Louise, examination of student work raised questions about the relationships between goals and classroom practice. Jen's attention to student work steered her to issues of communicating and language. She spent much time that school year thinking deeply about how content and language were interwoven in the learning of science and in experimenting with the idea that attention to language could actually be a way of learning science for some students. Language emerged as crucial to Louise as well, but in a different way. She dedicated time to discussing and refining the role that language and detailed explanation play in science. In response to a student comment, "But people don't talk this way, they are not that specific," Louise responded to the class, "No, you are right, in real life no one would talk to you if you always talked like that. But there are times when this is absolutely necessary. Someone said, 'This is so picky.' Well, that is true. Science is very picky; you have to be accurate. And you have to know the meanings of the words you use. Be excessively picky today."

While Louise valued the role language plays in learning, her attention to it was less explicit than was the case in Jen's teaching. Jen's attention to written language contributed to increased attention to words and how they string together to frame an argument. Louise's focus led her to pay more attention to the meaning underlying the words students used, to the point of questioning understanding when students provided her with the very words she had initially wanted to hear as evidence of understanding (good data vary).

Information gathered from student work informed future teaching and influenced classroom practice for both teachers. Jen had to plan for lots of time to accommodate the focus on writing. It wrought fundamental changes in her curriculum and instruction, in the nature of what she taught, and how she taught it. What Louise learned from student work influenced her teaching in essential ways, too. She used this information to organize curriculum and to decide what to teach. She changed what she formally assessed in order to obtain information that would give her an idea of the sense her students were making of what they were learning in her classroom.

How Louise and Jen taught and the actions they took were reflections of who they were as teachers and as people, and what they held important. We see in their stories that their decisions and actions were strongly influenced by the goals they set for their students as well as for themselves. Louise came to the classroom with a vision of science developed in 22 years of practicing lab science in industry. Her view of science, based in her experience, permeated how she selected curriculum, what she chose to emphasize, and how she taught it. Jen's practice was guided by a belief that all her students could learn, and later, that they should learn to articulate their comprehension in writing. This informed her as she identified and implemented goals for her students in the classroom, such as the ability to articulate their understanding through narrative. By means of a dynamic interaction among beliefs, pedagogy, and examination of student work, Jen became clearer about what it means to be able to articulate one's understandings clearly in the science classroom.

Issues of context matter, too. Jen taught in a school dedicated to preparing students from a low-SES area for college. Cultivating communication skills was an important outcome, and as such stood as a schoolwide learning aim. Jen had small classes, which met as block periods, providing time for extensive one-on-one work. Louise worked within a large science department in a large public school (the largest middle school in the city), and taught five classes of 30 or more students. Both teachers had to negotiate expectations of parents and students. Many of the students in Louise's honors class, for example, initially resisted assessment procedures that did not privilege "getting it right." Additionally, parents expected to see scores or grades on school work their child brought home, rather than (or in addition to) comments and questions.

Though this chapter has focused on Jen and Louise, student work played a variety of roles in the assessment practices of all the teachers in CAPITAL. Most notably, the work provided valuable insight into what a student understood and didn't understand. Student work also served as an opportunity to begin conversations about understanding, expectations, and quality with students. For purposes of our interactions with teachers, conversations about student work grounded discussions (between teacher and researcher, among teachers) and made talk about practice, goals, and achievement tangible and concrete. The students' written work provided both the individual teacher and the group of teacher participants the opportunity to take fleeting moments in the classroom and pause to examine them more closely. Moreover, it served as a basis on which to examine and challenge views and assumptions about what understanding looks like, and what it means for students to demonstrate understanding—an assessment goal for every teacher.

③

Shifting Dilemmas: One Teacher's Story of Change

I may want to be like them, the other teachers, but I'm not. I'm not them. I'm me, and I have to figure out what works for me.
—Irene

ASSESSMENT GETS TO the heart of the matter. What's important? What's fair? And what fits me and my students? Irene's comment captures several features of change that surfaced among teachers in CAPITAL: It is personal, context dependent, and deliberate. Teachers need to have a voice in what it means to modify their practice and how it works in their classrooms, or the change is likely to be superficial and fleeting, if it happens at all. Change is rarely linear, straightforward, or comfortable, as Irene's story suggests.

This chapter tells the story of Irene's efforts to reconsider her assessment practices. It underscores the frustrations and dilemmas that arose for her as she strove to match her practice with her vision. The process was confounded as her vision shifted during the course of examining her own classroom practice all through her time with CAPITAL. Irene was forced to navigate a landscape where the events that unfolded in her classroom were often in conflict with her views about teaching, learning, and students. She sought to give her students greater autonomy in learning and assessment activities, while she grappled with her view that such involvement might scatter the focus of assessment and dilute the high standards to which she held her students accountable. To pause and take the time to figure out what you want, why you want it, and what works in your classroom is no easy task for any teacher. For Irene, it was at once frustrating, daunting, and exhilarating.

IRENE'S INITIAL VIEWS OF CLASSROOM ASSESSMENT

Irene taught five classes of 7th- and 8th-grade science at a middle school deemed "high achieving" by district and state accountability measures. Her teaching strategy combined activities, lecture, and discussion. She held her students to what she described as high standards, and according to Irene, students saw her as one of the "toughest" teachers in the school. Prior to her work with CAPITAL, Irene's assessment practices were unexceptional. Although she drew on journals, oral presentations, peer and self-reviews, and longer-term projects that students worked on outside of class, tests and quizzes were the prominent features of Irene's assessment terrain.

Regarding her reliance on tests and quizzes, Irene said, "They need to show me that they understand it on a test. Otherwise, I don't know whether it is them or from classmates or parents." Implicit in her comment are Irene's strong views on fairness. She believed that all students should receive the same treatment in her classroom, and she tried to provide her students with uniform experiences. Her sense of fairness contributed to the privileging of student test performance as an indicator of understanding. Conflicts among the assessment strategies did arise when students who did poorly on a test demonstrated proficient knowledge of similar concepts on another activity. She explained she did not know how to reconcile such inconsistencies, and was of a mixed mind about whether she should even try, since she could not be sure if a parent or friend had helped a student on assignments done outside of class.

The prominence of tests had other explanations as well. Irene felt responsible for preparing her students for high school. To be successful, Irene believed, students needed a solid foundation of content knowledge and needed to demonstrate that understanding through test performance. She felt that science teachers often sacrificed content to the processes of doing science. In her view, planning activities for students to "do" science often conflicted with planning meaningful learning experiences: "It is important to focus on learning rather than on activity for activity's sake. It's not just about the hook and experience. They need to learn the material." Irene felt strongly that processes should be embedded in what she considered important content.

Irene's classes, with the exception of one for English-language learners, had about 35 students. Her large class sizes and workload constrained what she could reasonably assign and assess:

> I have struggled to give meaningful feedback to students in a timely fashion. . . . I start off the year giving lengthy comments on assignments, but as the quarter progressed, students got their papers back weeks after turning [in] the assignment. . . . I have limited the assignments that I collect in which I write detailed comments. Most of the assignments, I have them complete in their books and [I stamp the notebook to indicate the assignment was completed].

Assignments that called for more creativity and critical thought were often sacrificed for assignments that could be graded quickly and more efficiently. She could speak of the value of high-quality feedback, but acknowledged that it was often sacrificed for marks based on completion of assignments.

IDENTIFYING AN EARLY ASSESSMENT FOCUS: CLASSROOM QUESTIONING

From the array of assessment issues that had arisen at her first CAPITAL summer institute (like feedback, peer assessment, quizzes, reporting, and grading policy), Irene chose to focus on questioning in her classroom. She wanted to examine in greater depth the nature of the questions she asked in class and how they figured in the flow of classroom life and learning. This focus was selected because it grew out of her interests, and also because it was a regular and important feature of her teaching. There would be little disruption.

Irene and a Stanford-based CAPITAL researcher developed a framework to look systematically at the questioning that took place in her classroom. Together, they examined her questioning practices and patterns during class discussions by considering the following:

- What question did Irene ask?
- What purpose did the question serve for her?
- What was the student response?
- What did Irene learn from the response(s)?
- How was the information used?

The researcher observed the class and took notes. Initially, analysis of her questioning patterns suggested that most of Irene's questions fell into two types: procedural and factual. Both categories of questions provided Irene with useful information about whether students had done their homework and knew what they should be doing in class. Questions like "Why do you press down gently?" and "Why do you need rulers?" before a seed-planting activity served to remind students about proper procedures. Factual recall questions (like "What are the variables we are testing?" and "What will a pod look like?") elicited information about whether the students knew what they should be looking for when they had laboratory materials in hand. Irene tended to look for specific responses that indicated whether or not she could move on in the lesson, whether students were ready to physically complete an activity, and what to emphasize in homework as review.

Subsequent conversations with CAPITAL staff and teachers about her use of questioning led Irene to articulate some of her beliefs and assumptions about the limits of classroom discourse as an integral part of assessment. Specifically, she was reluctant to consider remarks students made in class as evidence of understanding, particularly if this source of information would influence the calculation of grades. She identified numerous drawbacks to using information generated by oral questioning as evidence of individual understanding. Doing so would be unfair to some students, as not all students had an opportunity to respond to every question she asked; it would be a challenge to make sure that she polled all of her students so that none of them would fall through the cracks; it would be too complex and time-consuming to document and follow-up on responses; and it would prove difficult to devise an adequate mechanism to capture student responses in a systematic fashion.

While she was not comfortable using information gleaned in discussion for formal assessment purposes, consideration of the possibility created some dissonance. She recognized that students often could provide definitions for certain terms in tests and still be unable to apply their knowledge in problem-solving contexts. For instance, students could answer test questions like "What is a responding variable?" with prescribed definitions, yet many of those same students could not identify the responding variables in an experiment. These discrepancies brought home to Irene the gap between students' ability to verbalize a definition and the depth of understanding she wished to see. Irene began to reconsider what it was that tests and quizzes assessed and did not assess about students' understanding. Part of this examination entailed paying closer attention to other types of assessments that clarified what her students understood and might supplement what she learned from their test performance.

Over the course of a few months, Irene's questioning practices began to shift. Irene increasingly planned her questions for class discussions in advance. She became more deliberate in her questioning, more aware of the questions she asked and of her efforts to follow them up in the ensuing discussions. CAPITAL researchers who observed Irene's classroom noticed that she allowed more time for students to respond and asked more open-ended questions. These shifts did not occur overnight, nor was the change smooth or seamless.

During the transition, it was not uncommon for Irene to pose a question, and then immediately rephrase it, even before she finished her initial one. For example, before the class engaged in an activity to make pollination sticks, Irene's initial question, "Where will you find the stinger of a bee?," was immediately rephrased to "What role do bees play in the fertilization of flowers?" Only after a conversation about pollination did she return to the practical question about the anatomy of bees to ensure that students understood what they would be simulating when they undertook the task of making "bee sticks" for pollination. She began to seek responses from many students before responding herself, and she sometimes asked other students to respond to something a student had said. Irene began to organize class discussions increasingly around conceptual questions that she planned in advance to generate discussion and analytic thought, a significant shift from questions that had been primarily procedural in nature. Overall, her students became more visibly involved in classroom discussions, and Irene felt that student contributions became richer.

In a conversation with a researcher, Irene expressed enthusiasm for the quality of discussions that had occurred during a particular class. The students had begun a unit on the water cycle, and she had introduced the unit with a demonstration and discussion about density. She encouraged discussion by asking students to take a few minutes to reflect on the previous day's demonstration and generate related questions they still had. She was delighted with the responses, many of which indicated that they were engaging with the unit at a conceptual level. Examples included, "If materials expand when they get hot, why are rings difficult to remove from your hands? Wouldn't they expand too?" and "When you put a bottle of water in the freezer why does it explode if things contract when they cool down?" Irene commented to the researcher, "I hear all this good stuff in class during discussions so I know they are understanding material better than how they show me on tests."

This statement illustrated what was perhaps the most significant shift in Irene's teaching practice: a change in the way she listened to her students. Previously, Irene had listened for a certain response. The conceptual nature of her new questions, however, now required that she listen more carefully to what the students were trying to communicate. Irene observed that with a good question, "There are a lot of fruitful directions," and the same initial question took the discussion in very different trajectories in each of her classes. She was satisfied with the quality of the in-depth discussions and what she was learning from them about her students' understanding. But they took up class time. Faced with this, she knew that a tradeoff was necessary and she would have to reorganize her curriculum. She commented that while she covered fewer chapters in the text book than in past years, she was pleased to allocate class time for rich discussions that helped students build conceptual understanding and provided her with insight into what ideas needed review before time came for the test.

The dynamics of the classroom changed noticeably. Previously, dialogue often moved from student to Irene to student to Irene. Irene mediated all discussion; students spoke to *her*. With her new questioning strategies, responsibility spread among the class, with multiple students speaking before Irene responded. Students had started talking to one another.

FRUITFUL FRUSTRATIONS

Reconciling the Discrepancies Between Student Performance on Tests and on Other Assessments

With changes came new frustrations. Irene knew she could no longer ignore the apparent disconnect between test performance and understanding. She identified some thorny issues, which she proceeded to think about seriously:

> When I conduct oral discussions, some students are able to articulate well thought out responses, but when I ask a similar question on a test, the student does not express the depth of understanding that they demonstrate in class. Is it because of the prompts that I give them in class that assist them in their thinking?

She made several other comments that echoed this sentiment. "This year, kids who are doing well on tests don't seem to be getting it." She observed that the corollary was also true: students who did not do well on tests demonstrated understanding in the remarks they made during class discussions and in other aspects of their work. She also concluded that "on written work, more articulate kids do better." Irene conjectured that a different test format, such as an essay test, could alleviate some of the discrepancy between understanding and performance, but the amount of time it would take to grade a large number of essays made her reluctant to move in that direction. Instead, she sought ways to compensate. She evaluated homework for completion rather than for accuracy, a policy that dovetailed with her admission that it took too long to provide feedback to students in a timely and useful manner. Rather than a score, students received a stamp for completed work. The stamp converted to points in Irene's grade book.

Broader issues about what Irene could confidently infer from student performance and who was performing well were not so easily resolved. Discrepancies in performance raised questions about the quality of the information she gathered from her assessment system, how she used it to adjust her own teaching, and how that information contributed to scores and ultimately trimester grades. She began to question the validity of inferences she drew about student understanding.

Grades and Grading Practices

One of the areas that Irene examined was the meaning of her grading practices. All the CAPITAL teachers taught in schools where grades dominate assessment, and they continually revisited discussions about the meanings that underlie grades for them, their students, and their students' parents. The CAPITAL research agenda focused initially on the kinds of assessment that have a direct connection to the improvement of learning: those that help the student understand the nature of the gap between current comprehension and the level of understanding that is expected, and what might be done to close it. In spite of this focus, grades moved to the forefront in many conversations. Irene, along with CAPITAL peers and researchers, eventually spent significant time considering and discussing the interface between grades and understanding: What does a grade mean? How should grading and learning relate? How do they relate? How do we know what we know about a student's understanding? What information feeds into it? What isn't captured? What is important to grade?

Irene's ideal would be for a grade to reflect understanding of content, but she acknowledged that other elements were factored in as well. She saw her grades as reflecting the following:

- Mastery of subject
- Understanding concepts
- Completion of work
- Participation
- Projects, model, lab reports

While she desired a strong correspondence between a grade and conceptual understanding (as captured in the first two items she listed), she was no longer certain that this was the case in her classroom.

Through examination and reflection on her practice, Irene became convinced that her tests failed to provide her with an accurate or complete portrayal of a student's understanding. While Irene saw this as problematic, she felt initially that there was little she could do. Feeling trapped in a system where grades are the main currency, Irene acknowledged the anxiety students feel and the pressure on them to succeed. She shared her dilemma with her students and sought their feedback. She summarized their responses as follows:

> [O]ne of the kids in the discussion said, "Then just don't give tests," you know? It's like, We don't do well on tests, we do better on homework and in class work, just grade on those things. But then, you know, other kids said, "Well, in high school we are going to have a final exam, and it's going to be on the entire semester, and it is all based on a test." So, they know that they need to learn how [to take tests] despite the fact that they hate it. You know in a way they feel really stressed. And they don't like grades. They don't like this whole thing, but they are trapped in this thing too. Just like I am.

When a researcher spoke to students in her class, they spoke of the need to "get good grades, so I can get into a good high school, so I can get into a good college, then get a good job, so I can buy a house." Irene knew that the drive for good grades in her classroom often came at the expense of learning. The points and grades had become the end as well as the means, rather than representations of what students had learned.

In February and March of 2002, Irene repeatedly stated that she wanted to figure out how to shift the emphasis from grades to learning. She vowed to look for ways to link the two more closely. She had tried implementing different test formats, without finding a solution. She took time to consider how she could obtain assessment information from sources other than tests, and how this would look operationally. She thought that exploring those issues would be interesting and worthwhile tasks to pursue, setting the agenda for more focused attention and action. She articulated the new focus for her work in CAPITAL: "How can I integrate alternative forms of assessment into my teaching practice?"

She wanted to do so in a way that would make grades and performance true indicators of student understanding. In addition to continued attention to questioning, Irene's work with CAPITAL proceeded on two strands: (a) integrating into her teaching practice forms of assessment that provided a depth and dimension of information not present in her test-based system, and (b) helping her students perform better on tests. Both of these required that she reconsider students' roles in assessment to involve them more actively in the process.

Experimenting with Different Forms of Assessment

Irene sought ways to "reveal mastery of understanding" and, importantly, to do so in a way that would not overwhelm her with massive amounts of additional paperwork. She knew that some of the other CAPITAL teachers had experimented with an acceptable/ unacceptable policy for project-type work. (One teacher used this approach for all assignments.) The method was for teachers to share the criteria for "acceptable" with students in advance and for students to revise and resubmit work until it met the standard. These teachers shared their experiences and samples of student work that resulted from this approach with the CAPITAL group. They described improved performance by all students, including those whose past work had typically been of lower quality.

Elements of the acceptable/unacceptable policy appealed to Irene. She thought, however, that the approach would not work in her classroom. For one thing, she was not persuaded that it was fair to allow, in fact to encourage, students to continue to revise and submit work after a deadline without some consequence. "Isn't getting the assignment right the first time an indication of something important?" she asked rhetorically. "Should that not be acknowledged by the grading system?" She also had some logistical concerns, such as how to ensure that students would take the work and deadlines seriously if they had opportunities to redo the assignment for full credit. She said she liked the idea of revision, but was skeptical that she could find a way of executing it in a way that was fair to all students and that she found manageable. An initial solution to the increased load of "grading" generated by a process that required revisions was to assign group work. But, as noted earlier, Irene had not resolved tensions that she saw as inherent in group work.

After further conversations with some of the teachers who used the system in their classrooms with good results, Irene decided to reconsider. While she was not yet ready to embrace the new system entirely, she was ready to adopt aspects of it. The type of project work other teachers were doing in their classrooms was similar to what she assigned to her students, and she liked the idea of sharing evaluation criteria with students before they completed their work.

For her next activity, Irene decided to share evaluation criteria with students in advance. She asked students to design an experiment to figure out the conditions under which earthworms moved most quickly. She wanted them to design an experiment that tested one variable (e.g., light, wetness, surface type) while controlling all other conditions and to analyze the resulting data. She would provide students with wet and dry sand and plastic transparencies, and they could use the dry surfaces of their desktops. She would also provide equipment, such as flashlights, for students to use if they so desired. Her students had to complete a lab report, for which she distributed a rubric adapted from one used by a CAPITAL colleague for an acceptable/unacceptable lab project. She encouraged her students to use the rubric to assess their work before they handed it in to her.

An exchange with a student sparked questions in her mind about the students' ability to evaluate subject matter and the effectiveness of rubrics in helping them do so. Two of the criteria in the rubric focused on the hypothesis: The hypothesis needed to be clear, and it needed to match the conclusion. In his experiment, one of her students, Robert, had hypothesized that the worm would move faster on a transparency than on the dry surface of the table or in either wet or dry sand because there would be more friction on the transparency. After numerous trials, Robert found that the worm did indeed cover more ground in a given time on the transparency than on other surfaces, like the tabletop and sand. Irene pointed out that even though Robert's hypothesis was clear and corresponded with his conclusion, he should not get credit because his reasoning illustrated an erroneous grasp of content. He incorrectly used friction as the reason why the worm moved more quickly across the transparency. She explained:

> In his hypothesis there was an explanation of what he believed to be correct. And it was clearly written. But his hypothesis was something like, "The earthworm will be able to travel on the clear transparency faster because there is more friction." . . . I tried to ask him, "What does friction mean to you? It is not something I taught, right?" and he said, "Like if it is rough or smooth." . . . He said, "Actually what happened after we measured the speed, the one with the wet sand moved the fastest, faster than the transparency alone or the dry sand or the light." And I said, "well, is it really friction that you're measuring?"

Irene encouraged Robert to revise either his hypothesis or his conclusion before he submitted the work for a grade. Since his hypothesis was clear and related to his conclusion, Robert thought he deserved full credit without revision, as did his peers, who looked at his response in light of the rubric. She saw this as an example of the problematic side of alternative forms of assessment: "All this stuff is correct—technically speaking, according to the rubric—but it does not make sense logically."

She concluded that the accuracy (or quality) of subject matter was difficult to articulate in a rubric. Teachers could not anticipate the directions students' work would take or the topics they might address. Tersely stated criteria such as "Information is accurate" were too vague to assist students looking for ways to improve their work. Irene thought that those who used rubrics for assessment had to be careful not to sacrifice accuracy for making students feel involved with the assessment of their work. For this particular assignment, Irene accommodated her emphasis on content by adding 20 additional points—after the students completed and submitted their work—for "accuracy of information." These discretionary points were hers to determine. She continues to distribute rubrics in advance, with leeway for her to add or subtract points for accurate and thorough responses.

Her experiences with Robert and others during this activity highlighted a variety of new issues for Irene. One concerned the value of revision. On Irene's prodding, Robert did revise his work, and in the process learned something about friction, a topic not covered until the following year. She took to heart perspectives from other CAPITAL teachers that any piece of work, even the better ones, could benefit from an opportunity to improve it. She had now seen it firsthand. The incident also contributed to her growing conviction that her students did not understand some of the elements of what she considered good quality for their work.

Nevertheless, Irene decided to explore the feasibility of further implementing an acceptable/unacceptable scheme in which revision was an expected and integral part of the assignment. She still had many questions: What about the students who do less work at the beginning? What about the students who slacked off, waiting until she told them what to do to improve? What about fairness? For several months, she actively explored issues related to making the acceptable/unacceptable scheme work in her classroom. For specifics and guidance, Irene turned to other CAPITAL teachers who had made it work for them in their classrooms. She questioned them in depth about how they implemented the policy, including how they ensured that students did not see the policy as an opportunity to slack off. She examined their student work samples and rubrics.

Even though questions remained, Irene was encouraged by the insights she gained from the other teachers, and decided to try the acceptable/unacceptable grading scheme with an upcoming project on the elements, in which students had to write a children's story about an element from the periodic table. In Irene's estimation, the attempt fell short of success. The students displayed resistance to this new approach. Some did not take their first drafts seriously; they wanted to get immediate feedback on quality from the teacher, rather than using the rubric to decide what steps to take. The quality of the students' initial work did not meet Irene's expectations. While disappointed with the results, Irene refused to be deterred. In this sequence of trial and modification, she did overcome some hurdles. Significantly, she decided that it was more important that her students develop an understanding than that they do so quickly: "I now feel it important to understand something at some time. And it doesn't matter how fast." This view was a significant move away from her original position that there was qualitative merit in getting something right on the first try, and that this achievement should be rewarded. She became committed to the process and felt that through experimentation she would eventually find the version that fit her classroom and practice well. She planned to try the acceptable/unacceptable system again, perhaps earlier in the year, perhaps with a smaller project, and perhaps with more explanation to her students.

Helping Students Improve Test Performance

Irene did not abandon all tests, nor did she relinquish the responsibility she felt to help her students improve their test-taking skills. Even with efforts to integrate alternative forms of assessment, test performance and preparation remained a priority because, in her opinion, such skills were necessary for success in high school science courses: "Is that a good skill to teach? Should they have that skill? Well, all the high school teachers tell me their grades are based on lab reports and tests. Midterms and finals and that kind of thing. There are very few teachers [who] say, 'Oh, I will collect their homework and give points for accuracy.'"

From talking to students and parents, she knew that many students studied for tests but did not know what or how to study. Rather than spending time going over key ideas, they often spent hours pouring over minute, insignificant details. She took it upon herself to help her students become better test takers:

I would like to start requiring the students to keep a notebook of class discussions and reviews. I will write down the major questions that will be asked in class discussions, and the students will have to jot down notes on the class discussion. For homework, they will have to summarize the answers and write down questions they have based on the discussion. I would like to see if this helps test performance. The major area where students' grades could be improved is test performance. I need to teach students to study more effectively. I have not figured out what more I can do besides what I am doing already.

The notebook with questions never materialized, but Irene began focusing study guides around key conceptual questions. She thought this would help students distinguish big ideas from trivial details. Her desire to help students perform better on tests remained a strong interest. As the project came to a close, it became the chief focus of her work.

Involving Students in Assessment

In early work in CAPITAL, Irene learned about the research indicating that learning is enhanced when students understand the criteria of quality in a given assignment, and are then given the opportunity to gauge the nature of the gap between what they have accomplished and what is expected. The goal is for the student to begin to figure out what must be done to close the gap. She also read about the benefits of students' examining the quality of other students' work to help identify gaps and make suggestions about what might be done to improve quality.

Irene took the view, however, that involving students in assessment—either peer or self-assessment activities—would not and could not work in her classroom, with her population of students. She offered many reasons, including privacy-related ones. She surmised that students would feel bad if another student knew about mistakes. She also commented on the large amount of time involved, and questioned students' ability to make honest assessments. She shared stories of students who were embarrassed when they had multiple errors or performed worse than their neighbor. She was skeptical that students could assess their own work well. As she had learned with Robert, when she had provided the rubric for the lab report, students with weak content knowledge couldn't accurately assess the quality of their own work however well they understood the formal criteria. She also figured that to involve students in the assessment process might mean that she would have to compromise her high standards, something that was at the core of her professional and personal values.

Despite these sentiments, and after hearing other CAPITAL teachers discuss their efforts on this front, Irene attempted to bring some of the ideas to life in her own classroom. What this meant and looked like in her class evolved over time. During one peer assessment activity, she asked students to grade another student's completed assignment. She instructed the students to take out their green pens and put away other writing implements. She then went through the assignment and told the students the correct answer. After she provided each answer, she asked some students to read the wording of the answer on the work they were assessing to guide them in deciding how to score it. The class did not get through the assignment by the time the bell rang.

Another time she provided students with a grading scheme and gave them the 45-minute class period to assess long-term science projects for two or three of their peers. Students tallied the scores. Irene asked her 8th-grade student helpers to retally the scores in case the students had made computation errors, and then averaged the scores and entered the number into her grade book.

Irene was not pleased with either of these peer assessment activities. However, she continued to try to find ways to involve students in assessment. And with time, peer assessment became less explicit and more integrated with the fabric of her teaching. As part of a What is Life? unit, students worked in small groups on an activity in which they were required to describe in detail various random objects and reflect on characteristics of living things. As groups wrapped up their work at the end of the class period, Irene suggested to students who had finished that they show "your object and your writing, read your description [to other students] and see if they know the object." She encouraged them further: "Help each other. Get together with another group, swap papers. Edit for each other. Make constructive criticism." This incident represented a major change in Irene's assessment practices and her views and ways of involving students to a greater degree in the assessment-related activities in the classroom.

Other signs of change also appeared. When students solicited her approval of their work, Irene turned the questions back to them. "Are *you* satisfied?" she asked. Irene also began to ask students for evidence when they said something was good: "Why do you say that?" She no longer planned for peer assessment days but rather encouraged students to become involved with one another in conversations about how to improve their work before they turned it in. Irene continued to seek opportunities to involve students at this level—an important feature of their taking charge of their learning. In two years, students had moved from being scorers to being discussants and critics of each other's work.

These activities and the ways they played out in her classroom convinced Irene that what worked in the classrooms of other teachers would not necessarily be successful in hers. She knew that she had to make modifications to peer assessment to accommodate her internal operating framework and the particular context of her classroom. In addition to her avowal to integrate alternative assessments and help her students improve test preparation and performance, Irene added student involvement as a priority. It has become a central piece of her vision of teaching:

> I envision a classroom of students who are clear in learning objectives and who actively participate in class discussions and activities. . . . I would like the students to learn how to study by writing study guides; modeling with students and analyzing why some of the concepts are right on target and others are not. . . . I would like students to be able to take charge of their learning, and be more successful in class without being told. . . . Ideally, I would like to see my students becoming independent learners.

LEARNING ABOUT CHANGE

It was difficult to detect notable change in Irene's practices during the first year of the project. In fact, she seemed resistant to change. While most teachers in the project ventured to try strategies and protocols introduced by others—indeed, they had joined CAPITAL on the assumption that they wanted to alter their assessment practices—Irene listened skeptically. She would not accept an idea because it worked for another teacher in another context. Irene needed to immerse herself in ideas and figure out a way of adapting them to her teaching situation and her persona as a teacher before she put them to work in her classroom. Only after a year of deliberation did Irene attempt to adapt the acceptable/unacceptable system to her classroom. She was deliberate in her action. She tried to envision all the ways that ideas could play out before she tried them.

Through examination of her teaching practice, Irene became clearer about what was driving her actions, and how they played out in her daily teaching. As she considered her assessment practices more closely, she wrestled with issues of fairness, worth, subject matter, and evidence of understanding. As she modified and reflected on her practice, she reconsidered curriculum, content aims, and her own experience learning science. Irene's journey as a teacher did not stop at the end of her association with CAPITAL. She continued to try to find ways to involve students in meaningful ways in her assessment, in ways that honored her "high standards," that would work and be manageable with the 160 grade-driven students she sees every day. She still sought to reconcile various tensions in her day-to-day practice as she worked toward a vision of a classroom where active student participation is central.

Irene's story and the struggles she faced along the way posed many questions and challenges for the research team. She deepened our understanding of the nature of change by challenging our own assumptions about how it takes place and what it looks like in the process. She helped illuminate how slow and tentative deep change can be, and raised questions of how to accommodate these new understandings in our work with the other teachers.

Teacher Collaboration and Assessment: The New Haven Group

E LAINE, JONI, NEIL, Tracey, and Vicki joined CAPITAL in the fall of 2000. All but one, Joni, taught in the same middle school, which serves a diverse student population in the New Haven Unified School District on the east side of San Francisco Bay. This allowed us to follow the group's attempts to address matters of classroom assessment as a group, as well as following the individual teachers. These teachers experimented with a range of assessment possibilities before turning more focused and sustained attention to feedback to students and grading practices, particularly of project work. The group's route and the individuals' experiences further underscore the variation in practices that can arise from a common idea or starting point. For these teachers, change involved a long-term conversation focused on practice, which was always respectful of the adaptation and reinvention that was necessary when teachers took an idea and made it work for their particular contexts, priorities, and styles. (Reflections on what contributed to the success of their shared work, and what proved challenging, raise issues for dissemination, a topic discussed in more detail in Chapter 6.)

Several of the New Haven teachers involved with CAPITAL shared similar backgrounds and experiences. Elaine, Joni, Tracey, and Vicki came to teaching after careers as laboratory biologists, and after they had children of their own. By the time they joined CAPI-TAL, they each had several years of teaching experience at the 7th- and 8th-grade levels, primarily teaching life and physical science. Neil, who joined the group later, shared a sense of common purposes in teaching with the others and was pleased to find colleagues in his school who were willing to reflect on and work toward improving their practice. Involvement with CAPITAL was not the first time that many among the group had worked together. They shared a history as colleagues, co-planning, serving on district curriculum committees, and alternating in the departmental chair position. Even though Joni did not teach in the same school as the others, she regularly communicated with them through district meetings and e-mail.

Their similar experiences, backgrounds, and priorities contributed to relationships that extended beyond professional boundaries and provided the groundwork for the reflective and collaborative action that occurred in CAPITAL-related activities. CAPITAL staff worked less intensively with the New Haven group than with the individual teachers discussed in earlier chapters. During the school year, interactions were primarily through monthly meetings and e-mail communications. The group also attended 3-day summer institutes at Stanford University in 2001 and 2002.

THE GROUP'S EARLY WORK

The group began its work in CAPITAL by creating an inventory of assessment practices regularly used in their classrooms. The teachers considered the nature of the information they collected from their students and their purposes for obtaining this information. They also probed what they learned from this information about their students' understanding and about how they, the teachers, used the information generated from assessment. Their lists of purposes and uses were extensive, ranging from monitoring the completion of homework to generating points for grading, from checking for understanding to diagnosing areas that needed to be addressed further. From student work they collected, the teachers knew about the degree to which a student understood or could apply a concept or skill, sometimes through multiple means. Despite these insights, they reported that at times they knew little about what students were struggling to understand, and they discussed why that might be so.

This initial exercise led to further examination of the purposes driving their practices. Vicki, for example, began to question the value of the amount of student paperwork she collected at the end of each week to read, mark, comment on, and record in her grade book. Others in the group shared her concern that much of the work went unmarked for several days before being returned to students. They began to consider the usefulness and utility of the assignments and the meaning that the resulting grades conveyed to students. Collectively, they wanted to improve their processes for providing feedback to students in a timelier manner, while also reducing the paperwork burden they all felt.

The group's joint inquiry into what they called paper management issues led them gradually to the educational goal of providing more timely feedback to students. The group's route was not predictable or uniform. While Tracey began to explore the use of weekly quizzes aligned to instructional goals as a means of focusing instruction, others began to revisit and learn from existing and former strategies.

Several of the teachers gravitated toward a reexamination of the Question of the Day warm-up, a prompt for students to tackle at the start of each class. In prior years, several of the teachers used the time while students were working on the Question of the Day for routine activities, like taking attendance or returning corrected work. Others in the group had dropped the practice in favor of additional instructional time. Vicki described her focus on developing questions that could generate information that would help her modify her teaching and instructional activities. She no longer used the Question of the Day to create a time for her to take care of classroom business; rather, she designed it as a way for her to gain immediate insight into students' understandings, so that she could alter her teaching accordingly. Eighteen months into the CAPITAL project, all the New Haven teachers regularly used a variation of the Question of the Day. Tracey replaced her weekly quiz with a daily question, as did some of the others.

The influence that the group members had on one another had become evident early in CAPITAL. They brought new ideas to the meetings and adapted others' ideas into their exploration of practice in their individual classrooms. But influence did not come solely from within the New Haven group. At the CAPITAL summer institute in 2001, Joe, one of the San Francisco teachers, described his efforts to help students work on their class assignments until he judged the work to be acceptable. Joe explained his rationale for his policy of revision and resubmission of work as providing the students the opportunity to demonstrate that they had mastered the concepts or skills, regardless of how long it took them to do so. Vicki was immediately intrigued with this idea and began her 2001–02 school year by instituting a similar strategy for the assessment of project work in her classroom. She called this her acceptable/not acceptable assessment. (We have already noted that Irene was intrigued by this possibility and also experimented with the idea.) "Acceptable" meant that the student had achieved the standards established for the project. "Not acceptable" meant that the assignment would need to be revised until it was judged to be acceptable. There was no middle ground. Either the standards were met, or they were not. Vicki explained her rationale for shaping and implementing this assessment strategy in her classroom: "I think that if something is worth learning in my class, I should make sure that everyone in the class has been given a chance to learn it and revisit it if they didn't learn it." She drew upon her previous year's work in developing explicit, adequately detailed rubrics and her strategies for helping the students to understand the criteria for quality as she embarked on this new approach.

In their second year with CAPITAL, all the teachers in the New Haven group instituted this strategy for assessing projects. As this approach spread through the group, each teacher made modifications to tailor the approach to his or her own practice. In the group conversations, the teachers described this assessment approach as one in which feedback to the students was more consistent because the standards and criteria for the work were clearer and more focused on the essential conceptual understandings expected of students. Joni strongly felt that the revision process afforded by the acceptable/not acceptable assessment strategy provided a more equitable opportunity for learning for all of her students:

I have leveled the learning field. . . . This process allows those students to keep trying until I know they understand the concepts better. I have gotten some of the biggest rewards of my teaching career by seeing the looks of pride and smiles that come over the faces of students who had revised time after time and finally got it!

Teachers varied in how they implemented the strategy. For some, it was a means for assessing project work. For others, it came to embody their assessment philosophy. The quality of the work that her students began to produce prompted Tracey to begin to use an acceptable/not acceptable approach for class work in addition to project work.

Some of the teachers experimented with new practices in their classrooms less readily than others. Elaine described some of her reservations about the acceptable/not acceptable practice when the group first talked about it:

My colleagues in CAPITAL first started this assessment practice and I must admit that, in the beginning, I was reluctant to grade on an acceptable/not acceptable basis. I felt that it would not be fair to those students who completed their work accurately and on time to allow other students who needed to make corrections to earn the same grade. In our group discussions about this practice, the focus of the assessment of projects was also shifting more toward the demonstration of the concepts and skills and less on the aesthetic quality of the work. I had difficulty justifying giving a student who turned in an elaborate project that demonstrated much effort and time spent the same grade as a student who turned in a project that appeared to be done quickly with less attention to the overall appearance of the work. I feared that this new assessment approach would not provide the incentive to students to do the high-quality work that some of my high-achieving students produced, knowing that their grades would be based solely on the scientific concepts and skills and less on beauty and appearance.

Elaine wanted her assessment of student work to value the effort that students put into their work and to reward those who demonstrated care and precision with appearance and presentation. Others in the group had said that they wanted their assessment of student work to focus on the demonstration of understanding of the science concepts and skills. Elaine eventually used the acceptable/not acceptable approach in her class, with modifications to the rubric that allowed her to include the aesthetic components of student work in her final assessment.

As evidenced in the example of the acceptable/not acceptable assessment scheme described above, ideas within the group did not just move from one teacher to another. They also grew and developed with each new iteration, and took on different guises in different contexts. The teachers adapted the ideas to meet their teaching needs and situations, and they were developing their notions of assessment and how to use assessment to support student learning. The weekly quizzes discussed early in the project, for example, were not mentioned very much in later conversations as the teachers explored the new ideas and approaches in self-assessment and peer assessment.

CHANGING MINDSETS

For all five New Haven teachers, the general shift in thinking about assessment was toward making learning goals and expectations more explicit to the students. They moved from an emphasis on grading student work after it is completed and submitted to an emphasis on providing immediate feedback that helps the students achieve the learning goals. These shifts were significant. As with many of the other CAPITAL teachers, the New Haven group generally described how their assessment practices had become more deliberately embedded in their ongoing instructional practices, rather than being focused solely on end-of-unit evaluation or on grading completed projects.

Questioning strategies and oral feedback given to students during instructional interactions became more conscious and deliberate acts of all the teachers. Daily interactions with students became opportunities to give on-the-spot written or oral feedback for revision of student work. During laboratory investigations and class activities, the teachers found they were pushing students to think more about their observations and their understanding of the phenomena they were investigating, rather than focusing mostly on managing behavior and giving directions. The teachers found that their attention to ongoing assessment during instructional interactions provided immediate opportunities for revision and refinement of ideas, allowed them to identify student misconceptions during instruction, and emphasized learning rather than right and wrong responses.

Changes in assessment practices were accompanied by deeper shifts in ideas of teaching and learning. Vicki noted the change in mindset underlying the purposes she saw for the Question of the Day:

> I think it's interesting that we can come back around to old methods with new eyes. When I think about the questions that I used to use for Question of the Day, in a lot of ways they weren't different. A lot of times they were the "let's make sure you understand what we did yesterday" kind of questions. In my first years of teaching, I think it was, Well, they didn't get it; I'm so irritated with them. And now it's just this opportunity to not only say, "They didn't get it." It's, She didn't get it or he didn't get it, and I have to take care of that individually, and I think [it] takes a lot of practice to get to that point.

The teachers began talking about how their mindsets about their role as the teacher were shifting. At the start of CAPITAL, the teachers began with a fundamental desire to reduce the amount of paperwork they felt they had to maintain to be fair and consistent in calculating grades for students. The teachers felt trapped in a cycle of collecting homework and projects, grading assignments with the primary goal of recording scores in their grade books, and returning the marked papers to the students in a timely manner. As the teachers' conversations turned to discussing ways to make expectations clearer to students, and as their appreciation grew for what information they could glean about a student's understanding through daily interactions, they began to play different roles in their classrooms. As Joni said, she no longer saw herself as a *teacher*, which connotes to her a one-way interaction in which she tells her students what they need to know; she now prefers the role she plays as a *facilitator* or *guide*, continually monitoring student work and providing feedback as to the direction she thinks students need to go to develop their ideas further. Joni's experience was not atypical of the larger CAPITAL group.

Although management of paper and grade spreadsheets was still part of the expectations for the teacher, the amount of time spent on these activities was greatly reduced in favor of time spent on designing meaningful projects with clear standards, daily interactions with students in both one-on-one and whole-class discussions, and creating more opportunities for peer feedback and self-assessment.

COLLABORATION REVISITED

In reflecting on their work together, the New Haven teachers agreed that having the time and opportunity to share ideas and talk about their teaching in an analytical and reflective mode was invaluable in helping them move forward in their thinking and action in their classrooms:

> The opportunity to not only deeply think about our own practice, but to talk about it with trusted colleagues, allowed us to ask all those unasked questions, of ourselves and others. Eventually, we became very comfortable asking each other why we did things the way we did in our classrooms. This led to change in each of us, not just our classroom practices, but in how we think about our classroom practice.

Reaching a point where teachers felt comfortable asking tough questions of one another in the group conversations took time. When the teachers first began to bring student work and suggest innovations to the group, rarely did the others challenge assumptions about the value of the assignment, or even what students would learn from completing it. Upon reflection on their work as a group, the teachers identified numerous occasions when they did not ask important questions in the early stages of their work together. Numerous explanations could exist: It was too early in the group process to question the worth of what someone was teaching; the focus on developing assessment practices overshadowed the bigger questions of worth; the group wasn't sure how questions of worth might interfere with an individual's momentum.

For this group, the variety of strategies that they employed in their classroom explorations, including Friday quizzes, the Question of the Day, and self-assessing checklists for students, were important in helping them develop their thinking and understanding about how assessment operated in their classroom. The willingness of these teachers to continue trying new approaches to classroom assessment provided the energy that fueled the group. The teachers cycled through taking action in their classrooms by employing new approaches, and then reflecting on what they were learning about their practice, about their students, and about assessment in the group discussions. By discussing both the reasons that guided their actions and what they were learning from their actions, the dynamic interaction among reason, knowledge, understanding, and action was often present in the conversations, but generally impossible to tease apart. Vicki summarized the group's process:

> It is through our collaboration that we begin to understand
> what an art teaching is. One of us will come to the group with
> an exciting idea. . . . We will sit for long periods of time
> discussing the idea, down to the most minute details. Then
> we take the ideas back to our own classrooms. If we decide to
> use it, we'll change it to make it work for us. We then share
> what we did and how it worked for our particular students
> and within our teaching philosophy. Another change might
> be made in another classroom. Sharing ideas definitely does
> not mean that we all are doing it the same way.

Vicki's words highlight the variation seen in CAPITAL, in this case, within the New Haven Group. Her remarks underscore the importance of conversation and deliberation in enacting change. Teachers seldom have opportunities for sustained discussion focused on practice. CAPITAL was designed to provide opportunities for groups of teachers to share ideas and analyze classroom practice, without the expectation that all teachers would implement the same changes or develop the same innovations in their classrooms. Accepting, even encouraging, variation proved powerful. The New Haven teachers stressed their sense of ownership of new ideas when they themselves had decided which ideas would be implemented in their classrooms and how they would be implemented.

TEACHER CHANGE: RESISTANCE AND RISK

The New Haven teachers had opportunities at their school sites to influence other teachers. They met with mixed success. Some of the colleagues they engaged in casual conversation about their assessment practices wanted to hear more, even to try some of the ideas. Others said, "That would never work for me." When a district administrator asked the CAPITAL-affiliated teachers to work at their school sites and with other teachers in the school district, the CAPITAL teachers discussed what they wanted to share with their colleagues with regard to assessment. They reflected on their experiences in CAPITAL and the value they placed on the opportunities to shape the direction of their own classroom work. They concluded that even a full working day would not enable them to engage with their district colleagues in ways that would allow the latter to experience the deep feeling of ownership of new practices that they themselves had been able to develop in CAPITAL. Given this judgment, they declined an invitation to conduct a formal workshop session. They wrote:

> We declined because we felt that real change occurs only when the teacher internalizes it. That means the teacher needs to see that improvement could happen, and the teacher needs to be willing to try something new and make it work for them. Sharing a lot of techniques, no matter how important we felt they were, would probably do little good. Instead, we offered to lead a discussion about assessment and

model it on our CAPITAL meetings—not offering solutions, but listening to teachers talk about what they'd like to improve in their classrooms and encouraging them to try something new. . . . Getting teachers to talk openly about what they'd like to change or about what doesn't work as well as they'd like in their classes is difficult, but the conversation is much richer than when teachers talk about what works for them.

The teachers concluded that change does not come easily, and not through single-session workshops. The richness of their experiences and the sustained impact on their practice resulted from their meandering and opportunistic routes. For these teachers, change involved a long-term conversation focused on practice while valuing and encouraging variation among members of the group. The New Haven group demonstrated that change works best to the extent that teachers can make it work for them. For these teachers, as for Irene, Jen, and Louise (Chapters 2 and 3), the slow and stuttering nature of change can be at least partly explained by teachers' striving to take ownership of ideas and modify them to work in their own classrooms.

For the New Haven teachers, change was a risky venture, though a worthwhile one. At one of the last meetings organized by CAPITAL for the New Haven group at their school site, Vicki further reflected on the uncertainty she felt about the work at the beginning of the project and where she saw herself currently:

You know what I seem to be finding is that I feel like there's this huge change in me this year. It's almost scary how you can teach this many years and then suddenly feel like, I'm jumping off a cliff or something. Everything feels so different, and it's because of this stuff. And I just realized that the inability to ask the "why" of yourself—it really doesn't seem to have to do with how long you have taught. And that's the scary thing . . . that teachers who have taught for 25 years sometimes haven't trained themselves to ask themselves why. . . . I would like to think that I would have come to this eventually by myself, but I'm not sure that's true. . . . It's an exhilarating jump off a cliff, but it's kind of scary too. Several things . . . I feel really different this year. I feel that because of what we've been doing, I know my students in ways that I never did before.

The image of walking up to the edge of a cliff conveys the unknown nature of the work the teachers were doing as well as the risk of failure that the teachers faced when trying new approaches in their classrooms. The change process was not just about introducing new classroom practices. Vicki's description conveys how her thinking about her professional work changed, how her interactions with the students changed, how her collegial relationships changed, and most fundamentally, how she as a person changed.

By drawing the intimate relationship between what a teacher does and who the teacher is and wants to be, Vicki's remarks capture the personal nature of change. She makes an articulate case from one teacher's experience and perspective that dissemination tactics that merely offer a proliferation of strategies, even very good ones, cannot create sustainable change. Again and again, CAPITAL teachers led us to challenge conventional notions of teacher change and the dissemination efforts that typically are carried out to spread educational innovations.

Where Can I Make a Difference? Teacher Goals Beyond the Classroom

TEACHERS DON'T COME to a new project as blank slates. Those who chose to work with CAPITAL each had a professional life with its own trajectory before we met him or her, and would continue to have one afterward. Because CAPITAL was all about collaborative examination of teachers' practices with respect to assessment, we expected to spend almost all our time with the teachers on this topic, and we did. Nevertheless, we became aware very quickly of some of the teachers' specific interests and commitments beyond the customary borders of assessment, commitments that would continue to guide their careers long after we stopped working with them. Moreover, some of these commitments were outside the traditional boundaries of the classroom.

We decided to learn more about these predispositions. Teachers in any sustained professional development effort must integrate the activities associated with the new initiative into a broader professional framework, which is more personal, stable, and deeper than any particular project—even one that lasts for 4 years and attempts to dig deeply into some fundamental beliefs about their practice. This chapter describes how three of the CAPITAL teachers made those connections between an examination of assessment practices in their own classrooms and a longer-term and continually evolving sense of their professional missions.

TEACHER LEADERSHIP AT THE DISTRICT LEVEL: ANTHONY

Anthony joined CAPITAL as he was entering his 11th year of teaching in the Oakland Unified School District. The science curriculum was his main interest. For several years, he had participated in efforts that brought fellow science teachers together to discuss and enrich their classroom programs. These were voluntary activities, which often entailed visits to field stations and museums, as well as to one another's classrooms. He was a well-known figure among middle school science teachers in the district.

It did not take very long in the CAPITAL project, however, for the Stanford team and the other participating teachers to realize that Anthony had a very special passion, which accompanied and complemented his curriculum focus. It permeated his conversations; it was featured in his written reflections; it related to virtually everything he did when examining assessment practice in the classroom. He was deeply committed to a single overarching professional goal: using his knowledge, skill, and experience for the purpose of placing Oakland teachers themselves at the center of the district's attempts to make improvements in the science program.

Making a Case for Teacher Professionalism

Anthony had seen too many failed attempts at "reform" in this beleaguered school district that had been initiated outside the schools to change school programs, and then "disseminated" to the teachers. He found them frequently to be counterproductive—and wearying. As often as not, the new reforms quickly disappeared—sometimes in a single year—only to be replaced by a new initiative that would have a similarly short life. Enormous amounts of time and money, usually employing expensive outside "experts," were expended trying to persuade teachers to adopt new programs. But the programs often seemed to have little relationship to what the teachers themselves saw as their own strengths and the particular needs of the students in their classes. One destructive consequence of externally conceived and short-lived reform cycles, he believed, was an increasingly demoralized teaching staff, destined never to catch up. Anthony came to believe that the remedy was for classroom teachers to be involved closely in decisions to launch new initiatives, as well as to design and implement them. He was resolved to be such a teacher and to lead such an effort.

For the school district, improving students' test scores was a priority. Therefore many of the so-called reforms were initiated in the area of high-stakes testing. They aimed to get teachers to teach and students to learn in a manner that would improve students' test performance. Anthony held strong views on the subject of how reforms relating to testing should be pursued at the school and district levels. As part of his sense of professional obligation, he made his views known publicly—through letters to the editor of local newspapers, speeches, and op-ed pieces. This is a segment broadcast by a widely heard, local public broadcasting station, KQED, in San Francisco:

> Is this carrot-and-stick approach to school reform the only way? Are we even rewarding the best teaching? One way to look at our situation is as a choice between two models. The standardized testing model says you motivate people, teachers and students alike, by telling them exactly what to do, then rewarding them for doing it and punishing them for failing to do it. . . . An alternative model is one that emphasizes teacher professionalism. This model says teachers will do their best not when threatened or coerced, but when given support and the opportunity to grow. Teachers are and must be accountable. The National Board of Professional Teaching Standards suggests that accomplished teachers are responsible for the learning in their classroom. They need to be able to organize and present curriculum, to give feedback to students, to assess growth, communicate with parents and participate in a professional community of educators. This is how they are accountable. They are not bound and determined to raise test scores. They are bound and determined to

increase student learning, which is measured many different ways. . . . But the standardized testing movement is leading to the narrowing of instruction, dumbing down our classroom, dumbing down what is expected of teachers.

Anthony believed that teacher professionalism offered a strong counterpoint to the standardized testing movement. Teacher professionalism, he held, required that standards, instead of being delivered to teachers by an external authority, be established and "owned" in major measure by those who embody them: The standards need to reflect the values, beliefs, and aspirations of the professionals who embody them. Seeing CAPITAL's view of teacher responsibilities as compatible with and reinforcing his own, he accepted the invitation to participate in the program.

His stance on the importance of teacher professionalism led him to study for the teacher-supervised National Board for Professional Teacher Standards examinations. Completing this rigorous certification process, which goes well beyond state-level licensure, would add to his credibility, advance the cause of teacher professionalism, and help amplify his own voice when he spoke to audiences beyond his own classroom.

Placing Teachers at the Center of School Improvement

Early in his teaching career, Anthony had worked with the Full Option Science System (FOSS), a curriculum development team based at the University of California at Berkeley, where he had seen what teachers could contribute to school improvement. Over the years, he came to associate participation by teachers in school reform as a crucial aspect of professionalism, a cause to which he had become increasingly committed. Eschewing a career in school administration, he turned his full attention to working with other teachers to demonstrate what teachers are capable of doing to initiate change and make improvements in science programs.

Among science teachers, inside his school and in the district, his initial focus was on improving the curriculum by including first-hand science experiences for students, thus incorporating and expanding on what he had learned in working with the FOSS group.

He always was sure to keep school principals and central office administrators apprised of what was happening when teachers took the lead. Frequently he worked with administrators in the central office to secure the funds necessary to launch and sustain the programs.

At the time he joined the CAPITAL group, Anthony was a member of an eight-member science department in his school, four of whom were new to the school. Characteristically, he was particularly alert for new opportunities for professional development, and he was adept at factoring them into ongoing programs. With a Middle School Demonstration Program (MSDP) grant from the California State Department of Education, which he was instrumental in securing, the department had recently embarked on a school-based professional development plan centered around improving the life sciences curriculum, with a particular focus on the four new science teachers. The CAPITAL connection helped him to strengthen the assessment component that was part of an examination of curricular objectives and performance standards. Using MSDP funds, all members of his department became associated with CAPITAL in monthly meetings at the school to examine student work and discuss issues of quality and how to improve it.

Anthony went further. He capitalized on his previous work with other science teachers in Oakland to persuade the central office that for this subject, teachers could assume leadership in an ongoing effort to improve science curriculum and teaching throughout the district. Here are some of his reflections, written more than a year after the teachers had been involved:

> We have involved more than a dozen of the District's science teachers, from at least seven different school sites, and involved them in generating standards-based curriculum and leading high quality professional development, including taking responsibility for the District's School Improvement Program (SIP) process. We have sustained a high level of participation from all of the schools in the District. Last Wednesday, when almost no other curricular area held District-wide training, we led sessions at three different sites that drew about 70 teachers. . . . This work is showing that it is possible to sustain a community of learners at a

district-wide level. It shows a group of dedicated leaders can build a process that serves teachers at all sites.

Anthony understood that teachers need to establish credibility if the district is to rely on them for major improvements. One aspect of credibility is stability over time. If the short-lived district-initiated cycles of reform that led to discouragement of teachers and confusion were to be replaced, it would be necessary to demonstrate the staying power of a group of teachers determined to make changes in how they worked with students and with one another. If the district was to be weaned from a new superintendent/new reform mentality, it would be essential to demonstrate the potential of an alternative. He wrote:

> It doesn't make sense to demand that teachers be honored as leaders when they have not shown that capacity. So through the [curriculum project] teams, Caleb [a fellow CAPITAL teacher in Oakland] and I have tried to build a consciousness among teachers that we are capable of providing this leadership, through actually doing it. . . . This work is beyond my own leadership. That is the most exciting thing. We have three teams working autonomously, and leaders have emerged for each that are carrying forward in the spirit we have united around. I see this as a key time to press our advantage [with the District], as decisions are being made that will shape district professional development for the next few years.

Assessment in Anthony's Classroom

What about CAPITAL's effect on Anthony's assessment practices in his own classroom? Anthony continually examined and modified his everyday assessment practices throughout the period of his involvement with the project. It was these practices that were discussed when the Stanford researchers visited his classes and when he met with other teachers in the project. He tried new approaches to peer assessment, for example, and he was perceptive in his analysis of how the students reacted and how his pedagogical approaches might be altered for greater impact on his students. His conversations with peers were deliberative and searching about the subject at hand. He was self-critical, and helpful to others. He modified his own practices.

Gradually, however, the teacher participants and the Stanford-based team came to realize that Anthony was intent on relating his CAPITAL-stimulated growing understanding of everyday assessment to his broader view of his professional mission. CAPITAL was not a permanent part of Anthony's professional life. However salient, it had to serve the long-term goals toward which he had decided to direct his career. Yes, Anthony wanted to continue to improve assessment practices in his own classroom, and did. But he also believed deeply that greater teacher leadership is the road to lasting and stable change in the school life of students, and he systematically folded all his CAPITAL-related activities into that vision.

CONNECTING CLASSROOM TO COMMUNITY: JOE

> There are too many things that young people today feel powerless about. Their own education should not be one of them! They should know what they need to learn about, be active in gaining knowledge, not overwhelmed with being judged and graded.
>
> —Joe

A research and professional development project focused on assessment initially held little interest for Joe, as might be inferred from this comment, which was written during an early CAPITAL meeting. Nevertheless he had joined the group because of what he had heard about the work some of his colleagues had done in a Stanford project. In his view, assessment was synonymous with testing, and it was primarily a device for pigeonholing students.

A significant shift for him was the realization that assessment could be used to mean much more than simply grading. Joe attributed this change to his reading "Inside the Black Box" (Black & Wiliam, 1998b) at a CAPITAL meeting. In a discussion afterward, Joe recognized himself, in his own words, as "the poster boy for misguided assessment practices that were not only not helping my students but actually harming them and their learning." He acknowledged that although his assessment practices noted the failings of his students, he neglected to attend to them in his instruction. Like many of the other CAPITAL teachers, this shift from assessment *of* learning to assessment *for* learning was one that Joe was eager to make. However, like all the other CAPITAL teachers, he had to find ways to work with this concept in a fashion that resonated with his particular values and fit his own practice.

Assessment in Service of Learning: Making Change Work in the Classroom

Joe began to look for ways of incorporating assessment into his classroom so that it would always be tied to learning. As with several other CAPITAL teachers, he began to allow his students to revise and resubmit their work. At the beginning of each class period, Joe visually checked each homework assignment, usually a written paragraph on a speculative question such as, "How could scientists explain finding sea fossils on top of a mountain?" or "If we want our model cars to go further and faster, would it work better for them to be heavy or light? Tell why." Students who had not answered the question in an acceptable fashion received oral comments on how they could better phrase or support a quick revision of their answer, which Joe returned to check a few minutes later. Each written test was also revisable, with students allowed to get full credit if they returned the test with each answer corrected. Joe wrote about his rationale and motivation in reflections for CAPITAL:

> Teachers have asked, "Why not give grades and comments together?" This negates the positive effects of comments. My son brings home work from his elementary school that is graded with a number score based on a rubric. Once he sees his score he is done looking at that paper. After reminding him that he can still learn from the paper if he looks at the teacher's comments, he has told me, "It doesn't matter any more; I already got graded on it." Many students internalize the grade as a judgment of them and come to accept this image of themselves. The motivation to continue

working is minimal, especially if they have worked hard and received a D.

The story of Joe's work with CAPITAL was not one of his making large-scale modifications in his assumptions or beliefs. In most ways, his classroom practice was remarkably consistent. Instead, change for Joe during the years he participated in CAPITAL seems primarily to have involved efforts to make his assumptions and beliefs about learning explicit to himself, and then constructing links between his assumptions and their implications for assessment. More than for the other CAPITAL teachers, the changes that became apparent were less in his instructional approach and more in fashioning and adding substance to the compass that already drove his decisionmaking.

"More Than Just a Science Teacher"

In the final weeks of a 9-week project Joe's students were completing on rocketry, space, and astronomy, he described their overall progress in an interview. He noted that the content was challenging, the students were learning, their products were good, and they were enjoying themselves. Still, he did not seem completely satisfied. Responding to a questioner's probing, he finally commented, "Well, if I were just a science teacher, I would be happy." Indeed, this statement holds the key to understanding Joe as a person and as a professional. Joe saw his role in the classroom broadly and from several perspectives. He always was and wanted to be more than "just a science teacher." He felt that teaching science was most meaningful when it introduced students to their community and gave them opportunities to address issues that were central to their lives beyond school. Not surprisingly, his own practice of teaching science and the projects and assignments his students were required to complete constantly emphasized issues of social justice and community involvement.

It would be misleading to state that all of Joe's curriculum revolved around social issues. His class contained familiar projects on and experiences with tectonic plates, earthworms, and convection currents. That said, Joe actively looked for and seized opportunities to make his students more socially aware, and to include issues of justice.

An illustration is his project centered on Hunter's Point in San Francisco. This project explored issues of the environment and pollution, focusing on the Bay Area's most notorious toxic site. Joe approached the project with an agenda of the issues he wanted to cover: asthma rates in Hunter's Point compared with other sections of the city, racial composition of the area, housing conditions, toxicity of certain substances, and the Navy's role in contaminating the area and its efforts to clean it up, for example. But he was flexible about the manner in which they would be explored. Soon after starting the project, Joe decided to have his students develop a short video public service announcement. In his students' hands, however, the project grew. Several started writing more. Enthusiasm was high. Joe decided to center the entire project around the production of a film.

The finished film, running 45 minutes, was shot and scripted entirely by Joe's students, much of it edited by students at Joe's house on his computer. It included video footage of a field trip to Hunter's point, where they interviewed the person heading the Navy's cleanup efforts and, separately, a local activist, who provided detailed accounts of recent toxic fires at the Navy site. In between student reenactments of key interviews that took place off camera, they visited City Hall in a failed attempt to meet with the mayor, and interviewed other city officials who had power and responsibility over Hunter's point. They also interviewed local community members, including the mother of two infants who need serious treatment for asthma and a grandfather who lost his 6-year-old grandson to cancer (both cancer and asthma are overrepresented in the area). One of the students described her own experience of losing her mother to breast cancer for the class and on the video. Joe also allowed the students to include a lighter side: staging fake talk shows and developing a fake commercial for "Jobo be Gone," a spray bottle that promises to remove annoying people.

Throughout their work on this film, students had an opportunity to pose and explore questions about how environmental issues that are understood through science come to have a role in public policy. Their own efforts allowed them to experience the passions and frustrations felt by many of those involved in activist movements. The students experienced the disappointment of not being able to get an audience with the mayor and the anger aroused by talking with victims of environmental pollution. They also felt gratified when the film they produced was aired frequently on San Francisco's public access television station.

Social issues, then, exist in Joe's curriculum as explicit content, as well as in an orientation to subject matter. They also exist in what has been called the hidden curriculum, those aspects of a curriculum that teach and have a pervasive influence on students' lives but are not found in curriculum documents or course outlines.

Assessment for Social Justice in Joe's Practice

Joe's professional concerns revolved around social justice for all students and their families. When he began his work with CAPITAL, he was skeptical about assessment, seeing it as a means of labeling and punishing students. Through his work with CAPITAL, Joe began to understand the possibilities of defining and using assessment to support and further student learning. Joe used these ideas to further his goals of social justice, both in his work as a teacher and in his work with teachers. He copied the *Inside the Black Box* article to distribute to fellow faculty members to enhance the schoolwide discussion about assessment. In CAPITAL meetings, he spoke passionately, yet unassumingly, about his views on his students and their needs, increasingly using classroom assessment issues and related ideas in his talk.

In his resistance to separating science from the human world, Joe's work pivoted on social justice and equity. His constant critical examination of the use of his power in common teacher-student relations, his unique solutions to issues of equity in assessment, and his tailoring of curricular materials to emphasize social justice displayed a deep sense of who he was and what he stood for. Within CAPITAL, Joe was an admired and respected teacher who helped all the others to remember why they entered the profession. Joe also presented provocative issues around the idea of what productive change might look like, and how assessment could be a wedge for altering the everyday assessment so as to better support the learning of *all* students. Joe modified some of his assessment practices to help students understand how their achievement could be improved. CAPITAL's major influence on Joe, however, was philosophical, leading him to deepen his ideas about how assessment could better serve his students and help move them toward improved learning.

A DIFFERENT PATH: CALEB

Though we started with the assumption that the classroom was the place to focus our energies and that the change process would be driven by teachers taking action in their own practice, these assumptions were challenged by some CAPITAL teachers. Action was not always the most obvious entry point for engaging teachers in reflective change. One teacher, in particular, tried to work within our framework, but in the end his efforts proved frustrating. Caleb had taught in the Oakland Unified School District for 5 years when he joined CAPITAL. Even while participating in CAPITAL, it was clear that he drew much satisfaction from his professional activities outside his classroom, particularly working with new teachers and other colleagues at the district level on curriculum reform projects.

As he participated in project activities, Caleb tried several new strategies in his classroom. He focused on questioning strategies, examined the quality of his discussions with his students in class, and considered student goal-setting. But the new strategies faded quickly. While other teachers embraced attempts to make even modest change and struggled through frustrations, Caleb's periodic attempts to try new classroom practices did not stem from his passions; his new strategies never lasted long, and long periods of time passed in which other things happening in his life drained his attention from his classroom. Taking action in his classroom as a means of moving toward understanding did not appeal to Caleb's sense of how to operate as a teacher. He valued the order and consistency that his classroom systems offered him and his students. Tinkering with his practice felt uncomfortable:

> I chose to focus most of my time supporting new teachers, developing curriculum, and planning special events, such as

Family Science Nights. These were tangible and significant changes I knew I could enact within my sphere of influence. In some ways, these were easier actions to take because their results were immediate and obvious. The resulting rewards and affirmation became indications of my ability to teach. The benefits of reflection and working on issues in my own classroom were much more subtle and complex. They were less flashy and often go unnoticed by others.

In his second year with CAPITAL, project staff searched for other entry points with Caleb. They helped him examine his regular practice of posting weekly grade sheets. Issues surrounding grading practices had been part of Caleb's priorities since his first conversations in CAPITAL. Caleb could readily identify benefits of posting grades, such as motivation, providing more control for the students, making expectations clear for students, and instilling a sense of responsibility. The downside of posting grades, such as labeling some students as failures, setting up a pattern of nonsuccess, and not addressing the question of why some students repeatedly do not turn in their work, were less apparent to Caleb in these early conversations. CAPITAL researchers encouraged him to reflect on and discuss his rationale for continuing this practice. Caleb described his experience:

> Over the course of my second year in CAPITAL, I stumbled upon the topic of grades and began to think critically about the issues surrounding them. I have posted grades weekly in my classroom for years to keep my students up to date about their progress. Using numbers to conceal identities, students regularly checked their progress. This simple task of grade posting became increasingly complex as I reflected and wrote about the issues. The grade junkies, cheating, and valuing of grades over learning offset the tangible benefits of this type of "accountability." Soon after, I expanded my thinking by tackling the entire concept of how grades are situated in my classroom.

While this reflective exercise led to little change in his practice during the time he actively worked in CAPITAL, it raised questions about his teaching that Caleb took with him to graduate school. While he was earning a master's degree in education, Caleb had an opportunity to reflect on his former practice from a new perspective. In writing later about his years in CAPITAL, Caleb highlighted the importance of the shift:

> Was CAPITAL successful in working with me to improve my assessment practices? I am uncertain. Perhaps the project was too focused on assessment for me personally. I often feel guilty that I was not able to institutionalize changes in my classroom. . . . However, engaging in this process of deep reflection developed a deeper appreciation and understanding for the complex dilemmas in my practice. I believe this change in my thinking is much more significant than if I was able to make a particular assessment strategy work in my classroom.

"I also realized," he said,

> that good ideas become increasingly complex during implementation. For one and a half years, I struggled through half a dozen strategies only to realize that the idea itself is not enough to create significant changes in my classroom. The hardest part takes place as an idea is put into practice in a real classroom. At the time, I was subconsciously unwilling to put in the amount of time and effort to make these strategies work in my classroom. Perhaps I was blinded into valuing the easier "projects" with immediate results.

What Caleb took away from his CAPITAL experience was not a new arsenal of classroom practices or an increased repertoire of assessment strategies. In fact, the work he did with CAPITAL may not have had a discernable impact on his students during the time that he actively worked in the project. Yet as he continued to learn from and build on his experience in CAPITAL, there were other changes:

> My priorities have changed. I now value reflection over action, complexity over simple solutions. . . . When looking at

the larger picture, the project had a significant impact on my educational paradigm. The interactions with colleagues who shared ideas, the support of mentors who constantly challenged my thinking, and the opportunities to write and articulate my thoughts all contributed to my personal growth.

As a practitioner poised to do professional development work with other teaching colleagues, Caleb takes this stance of reflection with him to his work with other colleagues. For Caleb, the entry point for change was not immediate action. Rather, it was identifying a particular practice—grading in his case—and encouraging him to problematize, articulate, and reconsider underlying rationales.

CHANGE IN CONTEXT

All the CAPITAL teachers worked on assessment and change with the aim of improving their practice, but the changes that took place that could be associated with CAPITAL were anything but uniform. Yes, some of these differences related to the unique context at each school: different students and parents, different levels of resources, different district policies, and different colleagues. But beneath these differences were the beliefs, values, and evolving sense of self of each teacher. As we saw in the case of Anthony, change can be about leveraging opportunities to further professional purposes other than those inside the classroom. As Joe demonstrates, change can be a process of becoming more articulate about what you do and why you do it. And Caleb's story shows that professional development efforts need multiple entry points to ensure professional growth.

⑥

Revisiting CAPITAL's Goals, Theories, Accomplishments, and Challenges

T HE TEACHERS and researchers who collaborated in CAPI-
TAL shared convictions about the highly personal nature of
teaching; about the powerful role of context in what is taught,
and how; about how teachers take action to help students learn; and
about how discussions among teachers about their actions in the
classroom can lead to deeper and more enduring change in actual
practice. Our approach to improving assessment in the classroom
was shaped in collaboration with the particular teacher, taking into
account the constraints that seemed to influence his or her situation,
the relationships that particular researchers and teachers were able
to establish, and the general dynamics of the overall collaborative
research group. Predisposed to reject one-size-fits-all interpretations
and given the rare opportunity to work intensively with teachers,
we did not spend much time planning one-size-fits-all methodologi-
cal procedures to be followed when we were out in schools. Our
work with the teachers entailed being present in their classrooms
(sometimes for a total of more than 100 hours with one teacher),
being attentive when they elucidated their actions, and asking questions intended to promote opportunities for them to tell us about

the guiding theories behind their attempts to try something different. The procedures we used grew from the circumstances we created. We wanted only to avoid superficiality in our attempts to understand the changes that take place when teachers have the opportunity to examine their practices searchingly and collaboratively.

While we regularly discussed and revised our evolving approach to the research, the focus narrowed as we tried to come to grips with the links between our approach and our results. What did we hope to learn? What did we learn? If each participant influenced and was influenced by the others, what were the ongoing and shifting relationships among what we hoped to understand, our approach to the research, and what we think we learned? What did we do, individually and collectively, as collaborating teachers and researchers in a project directed toward action, and how did we do it? And how could we describe our approach so that others might make sense of it? We attempt to address these questions in this chapter.

One impetus behind our work was the compelling research on the influence that improving the quality of everyday assessment in the classroom can have on student learning (Black & Wiliam, 1998a; National Research Council, 2001). The form improved everyday assessment can take to positively influence student achievement and learning includes attending to questioning (Minstrell, 1992; Minstrell & van Zee, 2003; Davis, 1996), carefully considering the nature of feedback (Kluger & DeNisi, 1996; Dweck, 1986; Butler, 1987; Sadler, 1989), articulating explicit evaluation criteria (Resnick & Resnick, 1991; Wiggins, 1998), and involving students actively in the assessment process (White & Frederiksen, 1998; Wolf, Bixby, Glen, & Gardner, 1991; Coffey, 2003). We shared much of this research with teachers as it seemed to relate to their interests.

THEORETICAL DISPOSITIONS

A philosophical stance that favors encouraging and understanding variation among the participants dictated that we be intent on finding out as much as we could about the teachers as individuals and the personal theories that framed the contours of their practice. These personal theories are shaped by the teachers' sense of who they are and who they want to be. Key factors include their beliefs about education, about their own capabilities, and about their students. These beliefs, in turn, are influenced by the teachers' own values, experiences, and sense of the possible. Such theories and beliefs are often implicit, and they almost always are directed toward practical action in particular circumstances, even if they have more abstract origins. Furthermore, they often emerge for examination only as teachers take action in their own classrooms, and then puzzle about the results and the reasons. Our theoretical ideas clustered around three concepts: practical reasoning, local knowledge, and teacher professional development. They formed the pillars of our approach to working with teachers.

We favor a notion of practical reasoning that develops through experience and is directed toward action. People with practical responsibilities, such as teachers, necessarily use what they know and believe when deciding what to do in highly contextualized settings (Gadamer, 1975; Schwab, 1969). Thus practical reasoning is much more than understanding general principles. For teachers, it is quintessentially a matter of taking principled action. Teachers learn about themselves and the improvement in their practice, in part, as they reflect on what they have done and try to make changes. In this view, one's actions in given situations, the intentions that shape them, and knowledge of the local context that influences them are at the core of understanding what one does. Our approach sought ways to make the thinking behind teachers' actions more explicit and transparent.

Since practical reasoning emphasizes context, we almost always privileged local knowledge (Nussbaum, 1978; 1986) in trying to figure out how the teachers with whom we worked approached their responsibilities and opportunities. That is, we tried hard to find out what drove them, what particular circumstances were consequential for them, how they developed and used knowledge that directly affected their own practice. "What drives them" includes their professional opportunities and aspirations, and also their sense of themselves and who they want to be as persons and as teachers. "Particular circumstances" includes the actual students they teach and the students' parents, the professional traditions and expectations in the school and the surrounding community, constraints of time and other resources, unanticipated and unpredict-able opportunities and pressures, and the colleagues with whom they associate on a regular basis. "How they develop and use knowl-edge" includes the insights they gain from their own experience in the classroom and from others (including colleagues and special-ists), and how.

We share a view of teacher professional development that is con-sistent with our theoretical starting points. We believe that teaching is a highly personal endeavor; how we teach is a reflection of who we are, and teaching is shaped by strongly shaped beliefs, whether articulated not, about teaching, learning, and students. Teachers who reflect thoughtfully on their practice strive to comprehend the gap between who they are and who they want to be, as people and as professionals. As they understand the nature of this gap, they fash-ion and direct their activities to close it. In the process of becoming who they want to be, teachers modify their practice and enrich the way they work with students. We feel that deliberation among peers is an important feature of teacher professional development and that teachers must be supported by communities of like-minded col-leagues in order to reflect meaningfully about their actions in the class-room (Lave and Wenger, 1991; Taylor, 1971). Teachers' understanding is deepened when they reflect on their actions and discuss their ex-periences in a professional community with peers who share similar values and are trying actively to make similar changes (Atkin, 1994; Feldman and Atkin, 1995; Cochran-Smith and Lytle, 1999; Elliot, 1987; Hargreaves, 1998; Zeichner, 1994).

SHAPING AN APPROACH

Teachers identified aspects of their practice that they wanted to improve or learn more about. They tried new strategies that they thought might work for their students, they wrote about them, they met regularly with other teachers in the project to discuss what they were doing and consider criticism, and they talked regularly with the Stanford-based participants.

The themes that teachers identified as the focus of their research and reflection formed the nucleus of our work with them. Though all the teachers committed themselves to work on issues associated with assessment, there was considerable variation in the interpretation and centrality of that commitment. Some of the themes addressed by the teachers were directly assessment related. Irene focused on questioning in class discussions and on uncovering whether and how she might create more student involvement in everyday assessment. Louise used student work both to get a glimpse into what her students understood and to make future teaching and curriculum decisions. Jen embarked on understanding the role of writing in the teaching of science and integrating it into her classroom. However, in Jen's case and in those of many of the others, assessment became a vehicle to investigate the way curriculum and instruction played out in the classroom. Joe added more detailed feedback to his assessments as a result of his work in CAPITAL, but, most of all, he began to see ways of fostering his goal of fairness for all students. Anthony was determined to use opportunities accorded by the project to enhance the role of all teachers in an educational climate that was promoting ever-greater reliance on standardized, externally developed tests.

Typically, our point of entry was an attempt by a teacher to modify an aspect of his or her practice. We worked with the teachers so that they and the other CAPITAL participants would better understand the changes and their effects. We tried to fathom, among other things, the beliefs and assumptions associated with the teachers' actions, the nature of the change they were embarked upon, how it played out in their classrooms, and the challenges and constraints they negotiated along the way. These focal topics were always assessment related, although it often transpired that a deeper investigation of the assessment focus took the inquiry into realms of curriculum and teaching. The flexibility of our approach and our inclination to honor the decisions of the teachers required that we, as a research team, stay open to whatever directions seemed relevant to them.

Individual teachers were supported by researchers, and teacher-researcher teams worked intensively in classroom environments. Often the researcher's role was to collect data for the research project (and sometimes for a teacher's nonproject purposes, if requested), to act as a mirror reflecting impressions drawn from the classroom back to the teacher, and to raise questions and probe the purposes and underlying reasoning of the teacher's actions. The teachers were researchers, too: as they examined practice, tried new ideas and practices in the classroom, and reflected on underlying reasons and rationales for their actions.

We came to this project with a strong desire to expand current notions of sound educational research to include the knowledge generated by and with teachers. As a research team, we were sensitive to the differences in influence that exist between researchers and practitioners and, consequently, the divide that often exists between the academy and the school classroom. Consistent with our theoretical biases is the predisposition to blur the difference between theory and practice, between thought and action. As a result, we have been explicit about wanting to honor the theories of individual teachers as we sought to understand the foundations for their practice. Schoolteachers are no more capricious than professors or anyone else. All their actions have reasons. We would have considered the project a failure if we did not strive to illuminate and understand them—even to present them in their best light. Consequently, we were deliberate in ensuring and being explicit about the fact that the teachers we felt privileged to work with were never "subjects" of research. They were our partners in the effort to understand classroom assessment and teacher change, and, as partners, they helped shape the direction of the project.

The nature of each teacher-researcher partnership also depended on what the Stanford-based researcher brought to it, so each relationship was different. The dynamic between particular pairs of teachers and researchers evolved according to the predispositions and expertise of the individuals involved, common experiences, shared interests and passions, and the local contexts in which they found themselves. Stanford-based Savitha, with her training and experience as an English/ESL teacher was attracted by Jen's desire to focus closely on writing and how it interacted with the teaching of science. Janet, pursuing a doctorate that focused on the students in development of an "assessment culture," brought that perspective to her work with Irene. Misty, with a rich background in professional development on the East Coast before she enrolled in Stanford's doctoral program, was well positioned to work with the New Haven teachers. Other partnerships between pairs of teachers and researchers unfolded around similarly shared matters of mutual concern. Each of the relationships developed in its own fashion, shaped by the beliefs, assumptions, and experience of the individuals involved in it, as well as the particular details of the teacher's professional setting (such as class sizes and resource levels).

Typically, university-based researchers conducted classroom observations and met with the teachers afterwards to discuss the events that had taken place. In these "debriefing" sessions, the researchers probed, collegially but persistently, for the reasons behind the teachers' actions. Some of the questions sought clarification, while others sought to elicit a sense of what the teachers strove for and how those goals related to their actions in the classroom. These conversations provided opportunities for the teachers to make their thinking explicit, strategize, and plan for the steps to come. Increasing levels of trust characterized the development of teacher-researcher relationships over time. The conversations became more candid and revealing, for both teachers and university-based researchers.

WHAT HAVE WE LEARNED?

It may seem paradoxical to seek wide-ranging lessons from a project that so unequivocally emphasized the differences among the participants. What can be learned of general interest when no teacher's path to changing assessment practices looked exactly like any other's? Can there be messages, nevertheless, that might make sense to others who face similar challenges of assisting teachers in looking deeply at their own work in classrooms? We believe there are.

About Assessment

As we concluded the project, we remained convinced of the power of assessment as a professional development tool. Assessment is tightly interwoven with what it means to be a teacher. Questions related to assessment quickly get to the heart of life in classrooms.

What is worth teaching, and thus worth assessing? What assumptions and visions of teaching, learning, and roles and responsibilities of students and teachers seem to be in play? As we saw in Chapters 2 through 5, reflecting on assessment quickly spreads to other aspects of teaching, such as curriculum, planning, and management. Examination of assessment-related issues helps teachers identify (and challenge) their priorities and visions, and consideration of assessment-related action informs revisions of earlier views. Four years after we launched CAPITAL, we remained convinced that assessment—especially the everyday type we sought to explore—provided a fruitful starting point for fruitful examinations of teaching.

About Change Among the Teachers

From the departure point of examining everyday assessment, the teachers who worked with us traveled in varied directions. Irene began with questioning; Anthony, with peer assessment. Jen ended up spending most of her energy attuned to issues of language and articulation. Louise focused on data, sampling student work for indications of what they didn't know. Joe's commitment to social justice led him to use assessment to better support all his students and help colleagues see how they could do the same.

Irene's story epitomizes what we have learned about teacher change, though the path she took was not exceptional among our teachers. By the end of her involvement with CAPITAL, Irene had changed her views about assessment, as well as her practice. These were deep shifts, in her philosophy of teaching as much as in her practice. Irene became more attuned to the details of student work and oral statements. Over the course of her CAPITAL involvement, she became more aware of the interrelated elements of her classroom, more aware of how events string together in the course of a day or a week. Her work on questioning, for example, influenced both the nature of her class discussions and the quality of the information she used to assess her students' understanding.

For Irene, as was the case with many of the other participating teachers, change was slow to come but deep when it did. Change happened, in all the cases, not overnight, and not by teachers' trying something new they heard about at a meeting, but slowly and deliberately. It happened after carefully examining and anticipating every angle. It happened by *partially* incorporating ideas into practice after much thought. And it happened only when it made sense in the teachers' own classrooms, in ways that were consistent with their vision of themselves and the classrooms they wanted to create.

About the Risky Nature of Change

We worked with experienced teachers. They were accustomed to events running fairly smoothly and to being able to anticipate how the day would unfold. When they joined CAPITAL, they expected close examination of their assessment practices with a view toward making changes that would fortify student learning. Nevertheless, they tended to be questioning, even skeptical, when new approaches (like peer and self-assessment) were discussed. Introducing something new is rarely easy and seldom comfortable, even for those with many years in the classroom. The discomfort of trying new ways of working with students subsides only in retrospect, and only with the recognition that teaching is a never-ending journey toward a horizon that is never reached:

> Last year, or even two years ago, I was much more rigid in terms of how I thought of assessment. I thought of it as tests, homework, accuracy. And now, I'm trying to broaden it. . . . It makes it kind of nerve-racking though. (Irene)

Opening one's classroom door can be risky. It requires a level of trust in the stranger from the university (or from anywhere else). The risks involved in opening oneself to having long-held assumptions examined and possibly challenged can be unsettling, particularly when the directions in which this examination will lead cannot be predicted. And development of trust takes time. The route may become slightly easier when one has recognized the power and benefit of something different.

About the Dynamic Nature of Change

Our classroom observations over the course of the project challenge the notion that change is static—that once it happens, it is always there in the same form. Some changes took root, as was the case with Louise's grading policy. Others faded. There were other instances where teachers were quick to adopt a new strategy or technique that seemed appealing, but with the passage of even a short time, few signs of the technique seemed to remain. Prior to her emphasis on writing, Jen spent time working with students to help identify content goals and objectives. We saw few signs of the changes she had made when she moved her focus to writing. Even when change lasted in the classroom, it did not go unquestioned. Louise found it necessary to examine the messages her new policy sends to students about accuracy, and Vicki has wondered if the acceptable/unacceptable policy best serves all her students in terms of learning content. Rather than being deterrents, these self-imposed challenges to new practices served as the impetus for still more questions, and deeper probing.

About Change Outside the Classroom

We anticipated change at the level of the classroom and teaching practices of teachers, but it often went further and was broader. In general, CAPITAL teachers moved in directions and on levels where they believed they could make the most significant difference, whether in the effects on other teachers, in the attitudes of school administrators toward teachers, or by enabling students to begin to see ways in which they can improve the local community.

About Change Among the Researchers

We university-based researchers were profoundly influenced in our views about teaching and change by the project. We were forced to confront our own assumptions and biases about professional development. Given our predisposition to honor the priorities of the teachers, we continually strained to figure out the roles we could and should play in working with the teachers: To what extent should we try explicitly to direct the teachers toward specific practices cited as effective in some of the research literature, as contrasted with introducing such research results when they seemed clearly relevant to a teacher's individual examination of his or her own practice? And to what extent should we try to direct teachers *away* from pedagogical practices that the same literature indicated were ineffective or even counterproductive?

We didn't always get it right. As a research group, we deliberately sought to avoid issues of grading. Discussion of grades, we reasoned, and the prior research suggested, distracted from our emphasis on effective formative assessment (defined as assessment that informs the regular teaching and learning), and already occupied too prominent a place in assessment conversations. When teachers brought up grading practices, as they often did, we tried to steer discussion to other assessment matters. Still, teachers persisted. They brought them up as they struggled to make sense of how to better harmonize grades as expected by students and parents with other ideas about the benefits of formative assessment that were being emphasized in the project. Only slowly did it begin to become clear to us that the teachers were not making the kinds of distinctions between formative and summative assessment found in the research and professional literature. Grades were a powerful fact of these teachers' lives, and they could not dissociate them from other elements of assessment.

Eventually we tackled the issue of grading head on. For 2 consecutive months, we urged CAPITAL teachers to reflect on their grading practices—to consider what grades meant, what they, the teachers, wanted them to mean, their place in the classroom, and students' perceptions of their meaning and place. We encouraged discussion about the many links between formative and summative assessment: To what extent is formative assessment an early indication of summative assessment? And can summative assessment be used for formative purposes? It was only after this concerted focus and discussion that we began to see more innovative grading practices, like the rapid spread through the project of acceptable/unacceptable evaluations, which blur the distinction between formative and summative assessment. Looking back, we realize that we as researchers were making distinctions that had little meaning for teachers. Parenthetically, our colleagues in the complementary project based at King's College London were coming to the same conclusion.

This influence occurred on an individual level as well as with the research team as a whole. Irene, for example, resisted Janet's persistent efforts to raise the issue of the role students were playing and could play in assessment. Janet's own doctoral research indicated that students could be involved actively and meaningfully, enhancing their understanding of what it means to do quality work. Irene's resistance was thoughtful and strong. She countered Janet's arguments with questions about, for example, the adequacy of students' knowledge of science. Janet left the experience with a more nuanced understanding of the setting in which Irene worked and with greater appreciation for the interconnectedness of philosophy, content, and assessment.

Through our close association with their activities, we learned that for our teachers, part of figuring out what could work in their classrooms involved figuring out who they wanted to be as teachers. In the process, they were redefining how they taught and what it meant for them to teach. On one level, it is difficult to make connections among beliefs, visions, assumptions, experiences, and actions. To purposely and confidently connect specific actions with beliefs and vice versa can be to ignore the complexity of any particular situation. The teachers helped us to understand the evolving and dynamic nature of teachers' assumptions and beliefs as they wrestle day after day with the fluid nature of classroom life. Our views of teachers' practical reasoning, one of the touchstones of CAPITAL, needed to be reexamined and deepened.

MOVING FORWARD

We learned a great deal from our teachers about what drives them, about why they do what they do. Teachers, too, can learn from articulating and reflecting on the very same questions. A success of CAPITAL was helping teachers and researchers alike make this connection between who they were as people and who they were as professionals. In any reform or professional development effort, the dynamic, bidirectional nature of action and change are central.

The CAPITAL experience demonstrates that certain kinds of educational change—if they are not to be superficial—call for deep knowledge on the part of the teachers of both the nature of the proposed change and the factors that drive their own practice. Change in the classroom entails much more than introducing teachers to new ideas and strategies. It requires settings in which teachers are encouraged to examine the new ideas, try things with their own classes, analyze what they have done, gauge the worth of suggested innovations in the light of their own goals and priorities, and figure out how the new practice might be factored into their full range of responsibilities. All this requires time—far more time than is usually provided for educational improvement.

The public hears regularly about successful innovations, like the powerful effect of formative assessment on the improvement of learning. It wants the new practice to be "scaled up" to benefit more students. Seldom, however, is there adequate understanding of what it takes for the new practice to spread to other teachers and schools. We believe we have learned in CAPITAL about some ways of working with teachers that actually work. We turn to these possible approaches in the next, final chapter.

Getting Practical About Teacher Professional Development

H OW DO WE DESIGN professional development programs that benefit students by building on the knowledge of their teachers? What conditions must be created for teachers to re-examine their practices if the public is serious about educational improvement? What must be included in the design if the changes in the classroom are expected to last?

Several features of CAPITAL emerged as salient in addressing these questions. They include a flexible starting point, a culture of collaboration and professionalism, a focus on practice, recognition of the teacher's own beliefs and goals, a reflective stance toward teaching, and enough time to enter a recurrent cycle in which teachers analyze, deliberate, and alter practice.

IDENTIFY A STARTING POINT WITH MILEAGE

- Find a focus that is important, that teachers care about, and that can incorporate varied pathways for improvement.

Though the CAPITAL territory clearly was assessment, the participating teachers held the compass for the journey. They had the latitude to move within that domain in the directions that most concerned them. So when some of them veered into curriculum, which initially seemed tangential to our goals, we took their lead. We tried hard to understand their motives, drives, and challenges—with the hope and expectation that they would show us the significant connection to assessment and the project. Almost without exception, they did.

CULTIVATE A CULTURE OF COLLABORATION

- Allow enough time for teachers to get to know one another.
- Facilitate relationships among group members, and provide opportunities for collaboration to grow outside of project meetings.

Collaboration was crucial in CAPITAL. As the teachers became more familiar with one another, they learned about the strengths and limitations of each person. Gradually they developed the levels of trust that are necessary for frank and productive conversations about one another's work. A culture of trust is necessary if participants are to be candid about false starts and serious doubts, as well as genuine pride and even exaltation. Such trust builds best on a combination of common purpose and mutual respect. CAPITAL researchers spent months in classrooms getting acquainted with the teachers and their teaching, and the teachers spent many hours talking with one another.

For some teachers, interpersonal connections were closer than for others, of course. The New Haven group had had a history of close associations, professionally and personally, which they built upon during their work with CAPITAL. But since productive professional conversations about beliefs and professional practices are unlikely to occur among strangers, congenial settings must be created for the purpose. (In CAPITAL, many of those settings included food, leading one participant to comment that "real" professional development is high-calorie work!)

SUPPORT A CULTURE OF PROFESSIONALISM

- Honor teachers' educational priorities. Accord them the opportunity to pursue pathways that are consistent with those priorities.
- Create opportunities for teachers to exchange ideas in a setting where differing points of view and commitments can be articulated and valued.
- Assist teachers in explaining their improvement efforts to colleagues, administrators, and parents.

CAPITAL teachers were committed to teaching and to engaging in the challenge of improving their own work. Likewise, CAPITAL researchers were committed to working collaboratively with the teachers as colleagues and professionals. We researchers strove to be partners and colleagues, even when teachers initially looked to us for advice, suggestions, and expertise. The participating teachers knew that we had all been teachers in elementary and secondary school classrooms ourselves; we knew that teachers have reasons for their practices, and we wanted to understand those reasons. Thus teachers' work and actions were always respected in our conversations. Under the terms of the NSF grant, teachers received stipends for their participation. Meetings were organized, run efficiently, and arranged around their schedules.

Sometimes change is risky for the teacher, not only because success is uncertain but also because colleagues, parents, and administrators can be skeptical about unfamiliar teaching practices. In the professional culture created within CAPITAL, reciprocity was important. When we occasionally had the opportunity to support the teachers with reluctant administrators, parents, and colleagues, we always did so.

FOCUS ON STUDENTS

- Organize discussion and reflection around questions that relate practice to student work.
- Use teachers' practices to help them challenge their beliefs and notions of the possible.
- Don't push too hard. Let trust emerge, and be alert for the occasions when the group is ready to challenge one other's actions and rationales.

One effective mechanism in CAPITAL for building a culture of collaboration and professionalism was to focus on the actual practices of the classroom teachers. While our agenda was fluid and contingent on the interests and directions of the participants, we encouraged teachers to bring student-produced material from their classrooms that would stimulate discussions. This allowed conversation to focus on student learning and work, rather than solely on the teachers' actions. We tried to smooth the establishment of connections among teachers outside of regular CAPITAL meetings, and facilitated non-project meetings when we were asked. We shuttled materials from one teacher to another during our regular visits.

DRAW ON AND FROM THE PERSONAL

- Provide catalysts for examining personal beliefs and expectations. One good place to start is with actual moves made by a teacher in a particular class. Why did she do that? What was she responding to? What did she see and hear as a result?

Much of what we learned about the nature of teacher change challenges conventional notions of dissemination. We are convinced that for the sustained and powerful spread of ideas, new programs or approaches need to figure out ways to honor the individual teacher's priorities, visions, and contexts. We know it is not feasible to expect the one-on-one relationships that characterized CAPITAL whenever an educational initiative is launched. Yet we also recognize there is much to be gained from investing the time and energy to build on the unique circumstances of each teacher when designing professional development experiences that are expected to make a difference.

The professional development that CAPITAL teachers experienced was based on their beliefs, it drew upon their professional and personal experiences, and it was greatly informed by their actions in their classrooms. Action was not merely the implementation of a new idea. It was the means through which the teachers developed understandings about their beliefs and assumptions. The change process that we now understand from our teachers does not support a notion of dissemination that relies on teachers "implementing" ideas presented to them by others. The apparent success of a particular innovation depends at least as much on the teacher as on the merits of a new technique or strategy.

As our stories confirm, teachers make scores of decisions every day. These decisions are guided and shaped by who the teachers are, and significantly, who they want to become. Louise chose to use data from student work in a particular way because she values certain kinds of information. She made decisions based on a mix of her own life experiences, what she believed about processes of learning, the discipline of science, and what she believes her students need. Jen worked very differently, informed and shaped by her own assumptions and background.

SUPPORT THE DEVELOPMENT OF A REFLECTIVE STANCE TOWARD TEACHING

- Make development of a reflective stance toward teaching a part of the program's goals and priorities. In many ways, this may emerge as longer lasting than the actual program agenda and focus.

In addition to improved classroom assessment, we saw changes in the CAPITAL teachers' orientations toward teaching and their profession. This was not accidental. By providing opportunities for teachers to examine their assumptions, and then act and reflect on that action, we conveyed a message about productive professional activity. Our aim was for this way of being and thinking about being a teacher to last well beyond the life of our grant.

We have seen evidence that this is the case. Irene joined a long-standing teacher-inquiry group offered through another university. A teacher in Oakland brought these priorities to his work as a professional development coordinator for new teachers. Even without the context of a project, Jen continues to experiment in her classroom, as do many of the others.

ALLOW TIME FOR EXPLORATION, REFLECTION, AND CHANGE

- Temper expectations about how quickly change will occur.
- Provide the time to experiment, backtrack, and re-group.
- Build recognition of the importance of time into project schedules.

Looking back on our work, we question whether the kind of deliberate and careful change we saw, with its stumbles and challenges, can be accomplished with great efficiency. Quite the contrary—classroom change adopted quickly on the basis of cursory knowledge of an innovation can turn out to be fleeting or superficial. It can even be counterproductive because it often is introduced by outside "experts" with no continuing responsibility in the school or district. Such dependency on outsiders can inhibit progress because it devalues teachers' own ability to initiate modifications of their own practice.

Our work suggests that professional development should focus primarily on the idea of development and come to grips with the necessity of recognizing that it takes time to make an idea or practice one's own. Propagating a new and promising idea certainly has its place in educational improvement, and can often whet the appetite of teachers by creating a new vision of the possible. But it must be internalized to be useful. Realization of even an attractive goal requires trial (and sometimes error) in the teacher's own classroom, and is enhanced by opportunities for discussion and experimentation with colleagues.

References

Atkin, J. M. (1994). Teacher research to change policy. In S. Hollingsworth & H. Sockett (Eds.), *93rd Yearbook of the National Society for the Study of Education, Part I. Teacher Research and Educational Reform* (pp. 103–120). Chicago: University of Chicago Press.

Black, P. J., & Wiliam, D. (1998a). Assessment and classroom learning. *Assessment in Education, 5*(1), 7–74.

Black, P. J., & Wiliam, D. (1998b). Inside the black box: Raising standards through formative assessment. *Phi Delta Kappan, 80*(2), 139–148.

Black, P. J., Harrison, C., Lee, C., Marshall, B., & Wiliam, D. (2002). *Working inside the black box: Assessment for learning in the classroom.* London, UK: King's College London Department of Education and Professional Studies.

Butler, R. (1987). Task-involving and ego-involving properties of evaluation: Effects of different feedback conditions on motivational perceptions, interest and performance. *Journal of Educational Psychology, 79*(4), 474–482.

Cochran-Smith, M., & Lytle, S. (1999). Relationships of knowledge and practice: Teacher learning in communities. In A. Iran-Nejad & C. D. Pearson (Eds.), *Review of Research in Education* (pp. 249–305). Washington, DC: American Educational Research Association.

Coffey, J. (2003). Involving students in assessment. In J. M. Atkin & J. E. Coffey (Eds.), *Everyday assessment in the science classroom* (pp. 75–88). Arlington, VA: National Science Teachers Association Press.

Crooks, T. J. (1988). The impact of classroom evaluation practices on students. *Review of Educational Research, 58*(4), 438–481.

Davis, B. (1996). Listening for differences: An evolving conception of mathematics teaching. *Journal for Research in Mathematics Education, 28*(3), 355–376.

Dweck, C. S. (1986). Motivational processes affecting learning. *American Psychologist, 41*(10), 1040–1048.

Elliot, J. (1987). Educational theory, practical philosophy, and action research. *British Journal of Educational Studies, 35*(2), 149–169.

Feldman, A., & Atkin, J. M. (1995). Embedding action research in professional practice. In S. Noffke & R. Stevenson (Eds.), *Educational action research: Becoming practically critical* (pp. 127–137). New York: Teachers College Press.

Gadamer, H. G. (1975). *Truth and method*. New York: Seabury Press.

Hargreaves, A. (1998). *International handbook of educational change*. Dordrecht, Netherlands: Kluwer.

Kluger, A., & DeNisi, A. (1996). The effects of feedback interventions on performance: A historical review, a meta-analysis, and a preliminary feedback intervention theory. *Psychological Bulletin, 119*(2), 254–284.

Lave, J., & Wenger, E. (1991). *Situated learning: Legitimate peripheral participation*. Cambridge, England: Cambridge University Press.

Minstrell, J. (1992). Teaching science for understanding. In N. K. Pearsall (Ed.), *Scope, sequence, and coordination of secondary school science: Vol. 2. Relevant research* (pp. 237–251). Washington, DC: National Science Teachers Association.

Minstrell, J., & van Zee, E. (2003). Using questioning to foster student thinking. In J. M. Atkin and J. E. Coffey (Eds.), *Everyday assessment in the science classroom* (pp. 61–73). Arlington, VA:.National Science Teachers Association Press.

National Research Council. (2001). *Knowing what students know*. Washington, DC: National Academies Press.

Nussbaum, M. (1978). *Aristotle's "De Motu Animalium."* Princeton, NJ: Princeton University Press.

Nussbaum, M. (1986). *The fragility of goodness*. Cambridge, England: Cambridge University Press.

Resnick, L. B., & Resnick, D. P. (1991). Assessing the thinking curriculum: New tools for educational reform. In B. Gifford (Ed.), *Changing assessments: Alternative views of aptitude, achievement and instruction* (pp. 37–75). Boston: Kluwer.

Sadler, R. (1989). Formative assessment and the design of instructional systems. *Instructional Science, 18*, 119–144.

Schwab, J. J. (1969). *College curriculum and student protest*. Chicago: University of Chicago Press.

Taylor, C. (1971). Interpretation and the sciences of man. *Review of Metaphysics, 25*, 3–51.

White, B. Y., & Frederiksen, J. R. (1998). Inquiry, modeling and meta-cognition: Making science accessible to all students. *Cognition and Instruction 16*(1), 3–118.

Wiggins, G. (1998). *Educative assessment*. San Francisco: Jossey-Bass.

Wolf, D., Bixby, J., Glen, J. III, & Gardner, H. (1991). To use their minds well: Investigating new forms of student assessment. In G. Grant (Ed.), *Review of Research in Education* (pp. 31–74). Washington, DC: American Educational Research Association.

Zeichner, K. M. (1994). Personal renewal and social construction through teacher research. In S. Hollingsworth & H. Sockett (Eds.), *93rd Yearbook of the National Society for the Study of Education: Part I. Teacher research and educational reform* (pp. 66–85). Chicago: University of Chicago Press.

About the Authors

J Myron (Mike) Atkin, director of CAPITAL, is a professor of education emeritus at Stanford University. He taught science for 7 years in New York elementary and secondary schools, and joined the faculty of the University of Illinois at Urbana-Champaign in 1955. In 1979, he moved to Stanford. He is a National Associate of the National Academy of Sciences, where he was a member of the committee that developed the National Science Education Standards and Chair of the Committee on Science Education K–12.

Janet E. Coffey is an assistant professor in the Science Teaching Center at the University of Maryland, College Park. She received her PhD in science education from Stanford University. In addition to her work in CAPITAL, she participated in several other research efforts to better understand the intersections of classroom assessment and learning. Before attending graduate school, she taught middle school science in Washington, DC, and worked as a National Research Council staff member on the development of the National Science Education Standards.

Savitha Moorthy has taught English and ESL in a variety of contexts for the last 10 years, in India as well as the United States. She moved to Stanford University in 2000 to enter the PhD program at Stanford's School of Education. She has been involved with the NSF-funded CAPITAL project since 2001. She brought to the project a particular focus on the ways in which language and science interact in classroom settings. She is currently completing her doctoral dissertation; her research involves the ethnographic study of adult ESL programs in community-based organizations.

Mistilina Sato is an assistant professor of teacher development and science education at the University of Minnesota. Prior to receiving her doctorate in curriculum and teacher education from Stanford University, she taught middle-school science in New Jersey. She has worked with teachers in a variety of professional development settings on issues such as inquiry and the nature of science; classroom-centered assessment; earth, space, and environmental sciences; action research; and developing science curricula. As a postdoctoral fellow at Stanford University, she served as the director of the Resource Center for the National Board for Professional Teaching Standards.

Matthew Thibeault is a doctoral candidate in curriculum studies at Stanford University. An active music educator, he teaches at the School of the Arts High School in San Francisco. He also works frequently as a jazz and classical bassist. Prior to entering Stanford, he was the elementary music specialist for the Portola Valley School District in California.

Index